Wedding
crochet

Wedding crochet

20 romantic & feminine
crochet designs for your special day

Sandy Powers

Photography by
Tara Renaud

SELLERS
PUBLISHING

Published by **Sellers Publishing, Inc**.
161 John Roberts Road, South Portland, Maine 04106

Visit our Web site: www.sellerspublishing.com
E-mail: rsp@rsvp.com

Design and layout copyright © 2013 BlueRed Press Ltd
Text copyright © 2013 Sandy Powers
Patterns and templates copyright © 2013 Sandy Powers
Photography by Tara Renaud
All rights reserved.
Design by Matt Windsor

ISBN 13: 978-1-4162-0912-6
Library of Congress Number 2013931237

10 9 8 7 6 5 4 3 2 1

Printed and Bound in China

Contents

Crochet Hook Sizes		
METRIC SIZES(mm)	US SIZES	UK/ CANADIAN
2.0	-	14
2.25	B/1	13
2.5	-	12
2.75	C/2	-
3.0	-	11
3.25	D/3	10
3.5	E/4	9
3.75	F/5	-
4.0	G/6	8
4.5	7	7
5.0	H/8	6
5.5	I/9	5
6.0	J/10	4
6.5	K/10 1/2	3
7.0	-	2
8.0	L/11	0
9.0	M/13	00
10.0	N/15	000

Introduction

The first time I picked up a crochet hook, my intention was to make a small afghan — little did I know that it would change my life; I had fallen in love with crochet.

Exhilarated from that experience, I thought I was ready to move on to something more challenging: an adult-sized sweater. Despite my enthusiasm, the result was comical. One sleeve touched the floor while the other was too short. But, I learned several important things from making that sweater: take measurements before beginning a project, check the gauge as you progress, and keep count of your stitches and rows. Lessons well learned.

It was a treat to create the patterns for this book. Seeing the designs come to life is always a joy, especially as I watched the pretty brides don a sweater, drape a shawl, or gracefully pin a veil during the photo shoots. Those moments were a reminder to me that weddings are about making memories and there's something special about a handmade piece that recalls the most important day of your life.

I designed this line of wedding patterns for all brides and I hope that the sweaters or shawls or veils you decide to make will add some handcrafted charm to your wedding and become cherished heirlooms to pass down for years to come.

Sandy Powers

Veil adornment and Headbands

Flower and Feathers
Bird Cage Veil

White Bird Cage Veil

Flower Headband

Flower and Feathers Bird Cage Veil

This beautiful feathered bird cage veil will look stunning on any bride.

Materials

- Aunt Lydia's Fashion 3 Cotton, 100% mercerized cotton – Color name Bridal White / Color # 926 / 1 ball
- 1 decorative button
- 3 feathers
- Hair comb – 4¼" long
- ½ yd veil material
- Tapestry needle

- **Hook:** US D/4 (3.00mm) Susan Bates

Skill level: Easy

Flower measures approx. 5"

Glossary of abbreviations

ch – chain
dc – double crochet
hdc – half double crochet
rem – remaining
rep – repeat
*rep from * to * – repeat in between the stars
sc – single crochet
slst – slip stitch
trc – treble crochet

Note: First sew veil material to hair comb as shown in step 1 of pictures. Set aside for now.

FLOWER

Round 1: With D hook and Bridal White, ch2, 6sc in second ch from hook. Slst to join. (6sc)

Round 2: Ch1, 1hdc, 1dc, 1hdc, 1sc all in same st as joining, *(1slst, 1hdc, 1dc, 1hdc) all in next sc* rep from * to * 4 more times to create 6 petals. Slst to join.

Round 3: Ch3, pushing petals forward, sc in between next 2 petals, in the back. (See photo) *ch3, sc in between next 2 petals, in the back* rep from * to * 4 more times to create six ch3 loops. (6 loops)

Round 4: *(1sc, 1hdc, 3dc, 1hdc, 1sc) all in next ch3 loop* rep from * to *

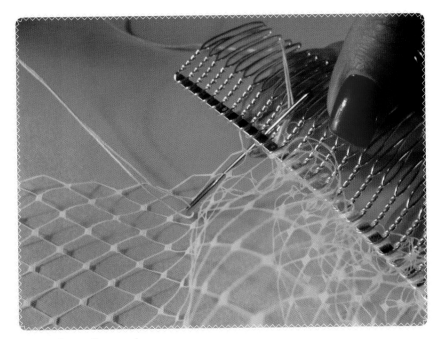

Step 1: Sew veil to comb

5 more times to create 6 petals. Slst to join.

Round 5: Ch4, pushing petals forward, sc in between next 2 petals in the back, *ch4, sc in between next 2 petals in the back* rep from * to * 4 more time to create six ch3 loops. (6 loops)

Round 6: *(1sc, 1hdc, 5dc, 1hdc, 1sc) all in next ch3 loop* rep from * to * 5 more times to create 6 petals. Slst to join.

Round 7: Ch5, pushing petals forward, sc in between next 2 petals in the back, *ch5, sc in between next 2 petals in the back* rep from * to * 4 more times to create six ch3 loops. (6 loops)

Round 8: *(1sc, 1hdc, 7dc, 1hdc, 1sc) all in next ch3 loop* rep from * to * 5 more times to create 6 petals. Slst to join.

Round 9: Ch6, pushing petals forward, sc in between next 2 petals in the back, *ch6, sc in between next 2 petals in the back* rep from * to * 4 more times to create six ch3 loops. (6 loops)

Round 10: *(1sc, 1hdc, 9dc, 1hdc, 1sc) all in next ch3 loop* rep from * to * 5 more times to create 6 petals. Slst to join.

Round 11: Ch7, pushing petals forward, sc in between next 2 petals in the back, *ch7 sc in between next 2petals in the back* rep from * to * 4 more times to create six ch3 loops. (6 loops)

Round 12: *(1sc, 1hdc, 11dc, 1hdc, 1sc) all in next ch3 loop* rep from * to * 5 more times to create 6 petals. Slst to join. Fasten off leaving a tail to sew with. Put aside for now.

LEAVES

Round 1: With D hook and Bridal White, ch6, slst to first ch to form a circle. Ch1, working all stitches in the circle, work the following: 2sc, 2hdc, 3dc, ch1, 3dc, 2hdc, 2sc. Slst to join.

Round 2: Ch1, 1sc in same st as joining, 1sc in next 3sts, 1hdc in next dc, 1dc in next 2dc, 3trc in next ch1sp, 1dc in next 2dc, 1hdc in next dc, 1sc in next 4sts. Slst to join.

Round 3: Ch1, 1slst in same st as joining, (ch1, 1slst in next st) rep to top of middle trc, slst in top of middle trc, ch3, slst in same st on top of middle trc, (ch1,1slst in next st) rep to end of round. Slst to join. Fasten off leaving a tail to sew with.

VEIL

Sew in feathers on comb where desired. Sew leaves to desired positions on rose. Sew rose to top of hair comb. Cut veil to desired length after you try it on the bride. Sew or glue decorative button in middle of flower. Pin veil with bobby pins to hold in place.

Step 2: Creating first row of petals

Step 3: Working in the back of petals

Step 4: Third row of petals

Step 5: Leaves

White Bird Cage Veil

A stunning veil that will add an elegant touch, and it's easy and fun to make.

Materials

- Cascade Sateen, 100% acrylic, 300.7yds/275m/100g
  – Color name White / Color # 6 / 1 skein
- Yarn needle
- Hair comb – 4¼" long
- Bird Cage Veil material ½ yd white
- 1 strand of white craft pearls approx. 1 yd
- Embellishments to go in center of flowers as desired

- **Hook:** US D/3 (3.25mm) Susan Bates

Skill level: Easy

Flowers measure approx. 5"

Glossary of abbreviations

ch – chain
dc – double crochet
hdc – half double crochet
rep – repeat
*rep from * to * – repeat in between
  the stars
sc – single crochet
slst – slip stitch
sp(s) – space(s)

FLOWER – Make 3
Ch6 counts as first dc and ch2 sp.
Row 1: Ch24, 1dc in sixth ch from hook, *ch2, skip next 2ch, 1dc in next ch* rep from * to * across. Turn. (7 ch2 sps)
Row 2: Ch1, 1sc in first dc, 5dc in next ch2 sp, 1sc in next dc, 6dc in next ch2 sp, 1sc in next dc, 7dc in next ch2 sp, 1sc in next dc, 8dc in next ch2 sp, 1sc in next dc, 9dc in next ch2 sp, 1sc in next dc, 9dc in next ch2 sp, 1sc in next dc, 10dc in next ch2 sp, 1sc in last dc. Fasten off leaving a tail to sew with. Roll stitches into a flower. Thread yarn needle and run a couple of stitches through the bottom of flower to hold it together.

Step 1: Row 1 of flower

LEAF – Make 3

Ch6, 1sc in second ch from hook, 1hdc in next ch, 1dc in next ch, 1hdc in next ch, 2sc in last ch, ch3, 1sc in same last ch. Now working on opposite side of ch, 1hdc in next ch, 1dc in next ch, 1hdc in next ch, 1sc in same ch as beg. Slst to join. Fasten off leaving a tail to sew with.

VEIL

Sew veil material to top of hair comb as shown in picture.

Sew flower and leaves on top of hair comb in desired positions. Push pearls thru slots in comb and weave thru slots around the 3 flowers to create the loops of pearls. Add embellishments as desired to center of flowers.

Weave in all ends.

Cut veil after you try it on the bride.

Use bobby pins to hold the veil in place.

Step 2: Row 2 of flower

Step 3: Roll the flower

Step 4: Run a thread to hold

Step 5: Leaf

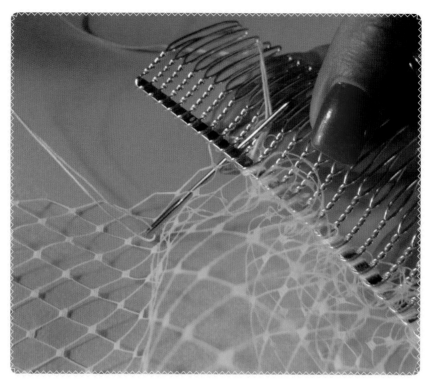

Step 6: Sew veil onto comb

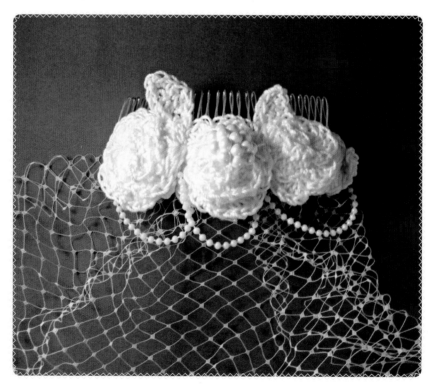

Finished article

Flower Headband

This playful headband in berry offers an opportunity for a fun splash of color.

Materials

- Kid Seta Noir, 25g/.88oz/232yds/212m
  60% Super Kid Mohair/22% silk/11% nylon/5% polyester/2%metallic
  – Color name Berry / Color # 15 / 1 skein
- Tapestry Needle
- 3 small buttons or embellishments

- **Hook:** US E/4 (3.50mm) Susan Bates

Skill level: Easy

Glossary of abbreviations

ch – chain
hdc – half double crochet
rep – repeat
*rep from * to * – repeat in between
  the stars
sc – single crochet
slst – slip stitch

HEADBAND

Cut length of elastic 1" longer than desired circumference of head. Overlap ends by 1", sew ends together.
Round 1: With E hook and double strands of Berry held together, work sc over elastic until elastic is covered with yarn. Slst to join round.
Round 2: Ch1, sc in same st as joining, skip next 3sc, *5hdc in next sc, skip next 3sc, slst in next sc, skip next 3sc* repeat from * to * around. Slst to join round, fasten off, weave in ends.

SMALL FLOWER – Make 2

Ch21, 3hdc in third ch from hook, 3hdc in each remaining ch, fasten off, leaving a tail to sew with.
Roll stitches into a rose, then run yarn through bottom layers to hold rose together. Take shank button, and using the tail, sew button into middle of flower securely. Sew flower onto headband.

LARGE FLOWER

Ch36, 3hdc in third ch from hook, 3hdc in each remaining ch, fasten off, leaving a tail to sew with.
Roll stitches into a rose, then run yarn through bottom layers to hold rose together. Take shank button, and using the tail, sew button into middle of flower securely.
Sew flower onto headband.

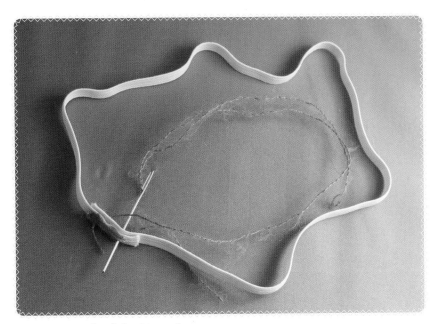

Step 1: Sew ends of elastic together

Step 2: Crochet around elastic.

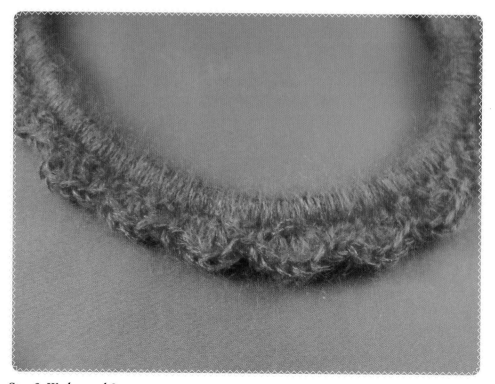

Step 3: Work round 2

Step 4: Roll stitches into a flower

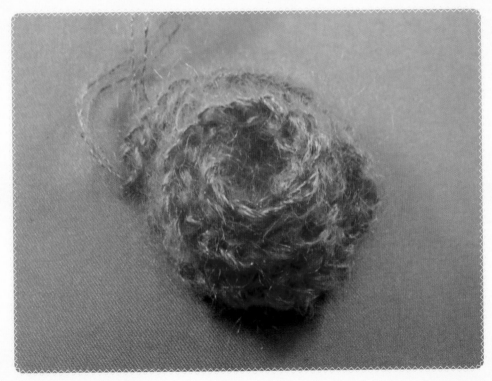

Step 5: Flower after rolling

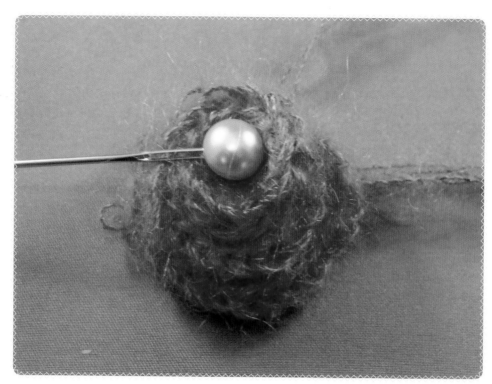

Step 6: Sew button in center of flower

Step 7: Sew flower to headband

Cardigans, Wraps, Shawls and Shrugs

Rosebud Shoulder Wrap

Elegant and Beautiful for any member of the wedding party to wear.

Materials

- Cascade Sateen 3.5oz/100g/300.7yds/275m, 100%acrylic, #2 weight yarn – Color name Sand / Color # 22 / 2 skeins
- Tapestry Needle
- Barrett
- 1 button or embellishment for center of flower

- **Hook:** US G/6 (4.00mm) Susan Bates

Skill level: Easy

Gauge: 2 rows – 1"
1 shell and 1 v-st – 1"

*Measures 34" (39", 43") long
for small, medium, large sizes*

Glossary of abbreviations

ch – chain
dc – double crochet
hdc – half double crochet
rem – remaining
rep – repeat
*rep from * to * – repeat in between the stars
sc – single crochet
shell – 5dc in ch 2 space
slst – slip stitch
tog – together
trc – treble crochet
v-st – 1dc, ch2, 1dc all in same stitch

WRAP

Row 1: With G hook and Sand, ch2, 3sc in second ch from hook. Ch1, turn. (3sc)

Row 2: 2sc in first sc, 1sc in next sc, 2sc in last sc. Ch1, turn. (5sc)

Row 3: 2sc in first sc, 1sc in each sc to last sc, 2sc in next sc. Ch1, turn. (7sc)

Rows 4–11: Rep row 3, increasing at the beginning of each row and in the last sc of each row, you will end with 23sc.

Ch3 counts as first dc.

Row 12: Ch3, skip next sc, *(1dc, ch2, 1dc) in next sc, skip next sc, 5dc in next sc, skip next sc* rep from * to* across, 1dc in last sc. Turn.

Row 13: Ch3, *(1dc, ch2, 1dc) in middle dc, 5dc in ch2sp* rep from *

Step 1: Row 12 of wrap

to * across, 1dc in turning ch.
Next rep row 13 until wrap measures all the way around the body to desired length. (See lengths above) minus approx. 2" so you can do the sc rows.
Row 1: 1sc in first dc, *skip next dc, 1sc in next st* rep from * to * across. (23sc)
Row 2: Sc tog the next 2sc, 1sc in each sc to last 2sc, sc tog the next 2sc. Ch1, turn. (21sc)
Row 3–11: Repeat row 2 until you end with 3sc.
Row 12: Sc tog the next 3sc, ch1. Do not fasten off but continue on to trim.

TRIM

Round 1: 2sc in each end of row on body of wrap and 1sc in each end of row on the sc ends. Work sc around entire wrap. Slst to join, ch1
Round 2: 1slst in same st as joining, skip next sc, 5hdc in next sc, skip next sc, *1slst in next sc, skip next sc, 5hdc in next sc, skip next sc* rep from * to * to point on other side of wrap, (first tie) ch60, (1sc, 1hdc, 1dc, 2trc, ch3, 1slst in top of trc, 1trc, 1dc, 1hdc, 1sc) all in second ch from hook, 1slst in next ch, 1sc in next ch, 1hdc in each rem ch, slst into same st as beg, *1slst in next sc, 5hdc in next sc, skip next sc* rep from * to * to point on other end of wrap, (second tie) ch60, (1sc, 1hdc, 1dc, 2trc, ch3, 1slst in top of trc, 1trc, 1dc, 1hdc, 1sc) all in second ch from hook, 1slst in next ch, 1sc in next ch, 1hdc in each rem ch, slst into same st as beg. Fasten off and weave in ends.

ROSE

Round 1: With Sand and G hook, ch 2, 6sc in second ch from hook. Slst to join. (6sc)
Round 2: (Sc, hdc, dc, hdc, sc) all in same st as joining, (sc, hdc, dc, hdc, sc) in each sc around to form 6 petals. Slst to join.
Round 3: Holding petals forward,

Step 2: Working up row 2 of trim

Step 3: Making ties

ch3, working in the back of the petals, sc in between the petals rep from * to * around 5 more times.

Round 4: (Sc, hdc, 3dc, hdc, sc) work all these stitches in each of the ch3 loops. Slst to join.

Round 5: Repeat round 3.

Round 6: (Sc, hdc, 5dc, hdc, sc) work all these stitches in each of the ch3 loops. Slst to join.

Round 7: Repeat round 3.

Round 8: (Sc, hdc, 7dc, hdc, sc) work all these stitches in each of the ch3 loops. Slst to join.

Fasten off leaving a tail to sew with. Add embellishments to flower if desired. Sew flower to top of barrette, then you can clip the flower onto front of wrap.

Step 4: Sc in between the petals front view

Step 5: Sc in between the petals back view

Step 6: Working in ch3 spaces behind first rows of petals to make second row of petals

Scallop Edged Shawl with Rosettes and Leaves

A sensational scallop-edged shawl, it is a perfect accessory
to keep the bride cozy while keeping a chill at bay.

Materials

- Paton's Beehive Baby Fingering, 3.5oz/100g/388yds/354m
  #1superfine weight, 70%acrylic, 30%nylon
  – Color name Angel White/ Color # 35005 / 3 skeins
- 6 assorted beads
- Beading needle
- Yarn needle

- **Hook:** US D/3 (3.25mm) Susan Bates

Skill level: Easy   **Gauge:** 32sc x 40rows – 4x4"

Glossary of abbreviations

ch – chain
dc – double crochet
hdc – half double crochet
rem – remaining
rep – repeat
*rep from * to * – repeat in between
  the stars
sc – single crochet
slant st – 1sc, ch3, 1dc,
  all in same stitch
slst – slip stitch

SHAWL

Row 1: With D hook and Angel White, ch81, 1sc in eleventh ch from hook, *ch5, skip next 3ch, 1sc in next ch* rep from * to* across. Turn.
Row 2: Ch5, 1sc in next ch5 loop *ch5, 1sc in next ch5 loop* rep from * to * across. Turn.
Repeat row 2 until shawl measures approx. 7 feet long. Do not fasten off but continue on to trim.

TRIM

Round 1: Turn shawl to long side, this will be your neck edge (where the collar will be) 5sc in first ch5 loop, 1sc in between next loops, *1sc in each ch5 loop, 1sc in between each set of loops* rep from * to * across to first

Step 1: Row 1 of scallop

corner, 10sc in corner loop. On the remaining three sides of the shawl: work 2sc in each ch5 loop and 1sc in between the ch loops and 10sc in each corner loops, ending with 5sc in same ch loop as beg 5sc. Slst to join. Do not fasten off but continue on to collar.

COLLAR

Row 1: Ch1, 1sc in same st as joining, 1sc each sc across top long side of shawl, to form collar. Ending with 1sc in first 5sc in last loop, leaving last 5sc in same loop unworked. Turn.

Row 2: Ch1, 1sc in each sc across collar edge only, working 1sc in first 5sc that are in the last ch loop, leaving the last 5sc from the same ch loop unworked. Turn.

Row 3: Ch1, 1sc in the back loop of each sc across. Turn.

Row 4: Ch1, 1sc in each sc across. Turn.

Row 5: Ch1, 1sc in next sc *ch7, skip next 2sc, 1sc in next sc* rep from * to * across. Turn.

Rows 6–9: Ch7, 1sc in next ch7 loop, *ch7, 1sc in next ch7 loop* rep from * to * across. Turn.

Row 10: Ch3, 6dc in next ch7 loop *5sc in next ch7 loop, 7dc in next ch7 loop* rep from * to* across, ending with 1sc in next sc, 4sc in end ch7 loop. Turn.

Row 11: Ch1, 1sc in next 4sc, skip next sc, 1dc in next dc, (ch1, 1dc) rep in next 6 dc, *skip next sc, 1sc in next 3sc, skip next sc, 1dc in next dc, (ch1, 1dc) rep in next 6 dc* rep from * to * across. Turn.

Row 12: Ch3, 1dc in same st as turning, (skip next dc, slant st in next dc) rep in parenthesis two more times, *skip next sc, slant st in next sc, skip next sc, slant st in next dc, (skip next dc, slant st in next dc) rep in parenthesis 2 more times *rep from * to * across. Do not turn, but continue on to instructions for short side of shawl.

Step 2: Row 2 of scallop

Step 3: Row 3 of scallop

Step 4: Working in loops behind petals

Step 5: Working in loops behind petals

SHORT SIDE

Row 1: (2sc in each ch loop, 1sc in between each ch loop) rep to bottom of first side. Then continue on to long bottom of shawl row.

BOTTOM SCALLOPS

Row 1: Ch3, 6dc in same st, *skip next 2sc, 1sc in next 5sc, skip next 2sc, 7dc in next sc* rep from * to * across bottom long side of shawl. Turn.
Row 2: Ch3, 1dc in next dc, (ch1, 1dc) rep in next 6 dc, *skip next sc, 1sc in next 3sc, skip next sc, 1dc in next dc, (ch1, 1dc) rep in next 6 dc* rep from * to * across. Turn.
Row 3: Ch3, 1dc in same st as turning, (skip next dc, slant st in next dc) rep in parenthesis two more times, *skip next sc, slant st in next sc, skip next sc, slant st in next dc, (skip next dc, slant st in next dc) rep in parenthesis two more times* rep from * to * across. Do not turn, but rep row 1 for short side of shawl. At end of row fasten off and weave in all ends.

FLOWERS – Make 6

Round 1: With D hook, and Angel White, ch2, 6sc in second ch from hook, slst to join. (6sc)
Round 2: Ch1, (1sc, 1hdc, 1dc, 1hdc, 1sc) all in same st as joining, *(1sc, 1hdc, 1dc, 1hdc, 1sc) all in next sc* repeat from * to * 4 more times, slst to join. (6 petals)
Round 3: Holding petals forward, *ch3, working in the back of the petals, sc around the post that is visible at the bottom of the petals* repeat from * to * 5 more times. (6 ch3 loops)
Round 4: (Sc, hdc, 3dc, hdc, sc) work all these stitches in each of the ch3 loops, slst to join.
Round 5: Rep round 3.
Round 6: (Sc, hdc, 5dc, hdc, sc) work all these stitches in each of the ch3 loops, slst to join.
Do not fasten off but continue on to stem.

STEM – Make 6

Row 1: Ch46, 1sc in second ch from hook, 1sc in each rem ch. Fasten off, leaving a tail to sew with.

LEAVES – Make 3 per stem

With D hook and Angel White, ch8, 1sc in second ch from hook, 1hdc in next ch, 1dc in next ch, 1trc in next ch, 1dc in next ch, 1hdc in next ch, 2sc in last ch. Now working on opposite side of ch, mirroring the stitches, 1hdc in next ch, 1dc in next ch, 1trc in next ch, 1dc in next ch, 1hdc in next ch, 1sc in last ch. Slst to join. Fasten off leaving a tail to sew with. Sew leaves onto stems.

Sew beads to center of flowers.

Sew flowers to short sides of shawl.

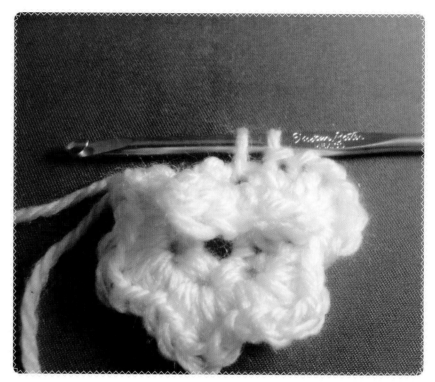

Step 6: Working second row of petals

Step 7: Working third row of petals

Lacy Cardigan

A beautifully designed lightweight cardigan that's soft and romantic and will keep her warm if there's a breeze.

Materials

- Aunt Lydia's Iced Bamboo Crochet Thread Size 3, 96% Viscose/4%metallic, 100yds/91meters
  – Color name Icicle / Color # 3001
  7 balls for small/medium size
  8 balls for large/x-large size
- Yarn needle
- 7 buttons – ⅝"

- **Hooks:** US D/3 (3.25mm) Susan Bates
  US F/5 (3.75mm) Susan Bates

Skill level: Intermediate

Gauge: 5sc x 4sc rows = 1"

Glossary of abbreviations

ch – chain
dc – double crochet
hdc – half double crochet
rem – remaining
rep – repeat
(RS) – right side of work
sc – single crochet
shell – 5hdc
slst – slip stitch
sp – space
tog – together
(WS) – wrong side of work

Note: Use D hook to make small/medium size
Use F hook to make large/x-large size
Ch3 counts as 1st dc

BACK

Row 1: With D or F hook and yarn, ch 86, 1sc in second ch from hook, 1sc in each rem ch. Turn. (85sc) The front of this row is right side of work (RS).

Row 2: Ch3, 1dc in each sc across. Turn. (85dc)

Row 3: Ch3, 1dc in next dc, ch3, (skip next 3dc, 1sc in next dc, ch3) twice, *skip next 3dc, 1dc in next 3dc, ch3, (skip next 3dc, 1sc in next dc, ch3) twice* rep from * to * across to last 5dc, skip next 3dc, 1dc in last 2dc. Turn.

Row 4: Ch3, 1dc in next dc, ch3, skip next ch3 sp, 7dc in next ch3 sp, ch3, *skip next ch3 sp, 1sc in next dc, ch1, skip next dc, 1sc in next dc, ch3, skip next ch3 sp, 7dc in next ch3 sp, ch3* rep from * to * across to last ch3 sp, skip last ch3 sp, 1dc in last 2dc. Turn.

Row 5: Ch3, 1dc in next dc, ch3, skip next ch3 sp, 1dc in next dc, (ch1, 1dc in next dc) 6 times, *skip next ch3 sp, 3dc in next ch-1 sp, skip next ch3 sp, 1dc in next dc, (ch1, 1dc in next dc) 6 times, * rep from * to * across to last ch3 sp, skip last ch3 sp,ch3, 1dc in last 2dc. Turn.

Row 6: Ch3, 1dc in next dc, ch3, skip next ch3 sp, 1sc in next ch1 sp, (ch3, 1sc in next ch1 sp) 5 times, *ch3, skip next 5dc, 1sc in next ch1sp, (ch3, 1sc in next ch1 sp) 5 times* rep from * to * across to last 3dc, ch3, skip next dc, skip next ch3 sp, 1dc in last 2dc. Turn.

Row 7: Ch3, 1dc in next dc, ch3, skip next two ch3 sps, 1sc in next ch3 sp, ch3, skip next ch3 sp, 1sc in next ch3 sp, ch3, *skip next ch3 sp, 3dc in next ch3 sp, ch3, (skip next ch3 sp, 1sc in next ch3 sp, ch3) twice* rep from * to * across to last 2sps, skip last 2sps, 1dc in last 2dc. Turn.

Rows 8–43: Repeat rows 4–7 in sequence.

Rows 44–46: Repeat rows 4–6 once. At end of row 46 fasten off and weave in ends.

SHOULDER SHAPING ON BACK
Back Right Shoulder

Row 1: With D or F hook and yarn, and working on the opposite side of starting ch, attach yarn to RS on row 1, 1sc in same st as joining, 1sc in next 29sc. Ch1, turn. (30sc)

Row 2: Sc tog the next 2sc, 1sc in each sc across. Ch1 turn. (29sc)

Row 3: 1sc in each sc to last 2sc, sc tog the last 2sc. Ch1, turn. (28sc)

Row 4: Repeat row 2. (27sc)
Row 5: Repeat row 3. (26sc)
Row 6: Repeat row 2. (25sc) Fasten off and weave in all ends.

Back Left Shoulder

Row 1: With D or F hook and yarn, and working on the opposite side of starting ch, skip next 25sts, attach yarn to RS on row 1, ch1, 1sc in same st as joining, 1sc in next 29sc. Ch1, turn. (30sc)
Row 2: 1sc in each sc to last 2sc, sc tog the last 2sc. Ch1, turn. (29sc)
Row 3: Sc tog the next 2sc, 1sc in each sc across. Ch1 turn. (28sc)

Row 4: Repeat row 2. (27sc)
Row 5: Repeat row 3. (26sc)
Row 6: Repeat row 2. (25sc) Fasten off and weave in all ends.

FRONT OF CARDIGAN – Make 2

Note: Both sides are worked the same until you get to the shoulder shaping.
Row 1: With D or F hook and yarn, ch58, 1sc in second ch from hook, 1sc in each rem ch. Turn. (57sc)
Row 2: Ch3, 1dc in each sc across. Turn. (57dc)
Row 3–46: Repeat rows 3–46 same as for back.

SHOULDER SHAPING ON FRONTS
Right Shoulder

Row 1: With D or F hook and yarn, and working on the opposite side of starting ch, attach yarn to RS on row 1, ch1, 1sc in same st as joining, 1sc in next 29sc. Ch1, turn. (30sc)
Row 2: Sc tog the next 2sc, 1sc in each sc across. Ch1 turn. (29sc)
Row 3: 1sc in each sc to last 2sc, sc tog the last 2sc. Ch1, turn. (28sc)
Row 4: Repeat row 2. (27sc)
Row 5: Repeat row 3. (26sc)
Row 6: Repeat row 2. (25sc) Fasten off and weave in all ends.

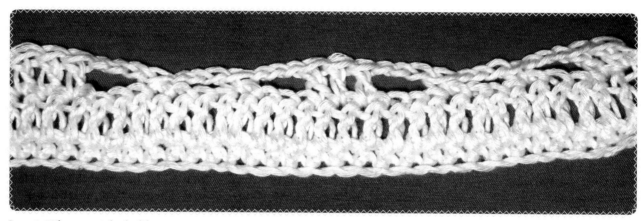

Step 1: What row 3 looks like

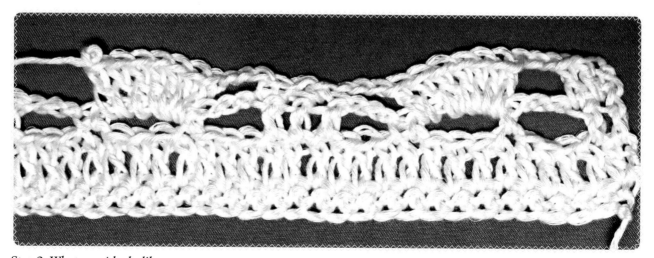

Step 2: What row 4 looks like

Left Shoulder

Row 1: With D or F hook and yarn, and working on the opposite side of starting ch, starting from the right, count over 27sc, attach yarn in next sc, to RS on row 1, ch1, 1sc in same st as joining, 1sc in next 29sc. Ch1, turn. (30sc)

Row 2: 1sc in each sc to last 2sc, sc tog the last 2sc. Ch1, turn. (29sc)

Row 3: Sc tog the next 2sc, 1sc in each sc across. Ch1 turn. (28sc)

Row 4: Repeat row 2. (27sc)

Row 5: Repeat row 3. (26sc)

Row 6: Repeat row 2. (25sc) Fasten off and weave in all ends.

Matching shoulder seams and with right sides facing each other, sc tog the 25sc for each shoulder seam. Weave in all ends.

Then holding a front and back tog, RS facing each other, starting at bottom of sweater, sc side seams tog. Work from row 46 up to row 22, holding sides so the stitches match, sc tog. Fasten off and weave in ends.

Then continue to armhole instructions.

Step 3: What row 5 looks like

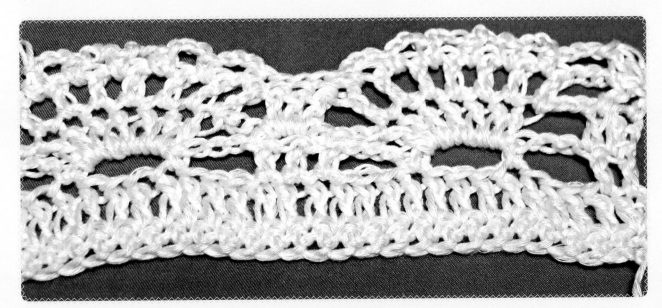

Step 4: What row 6 looks like

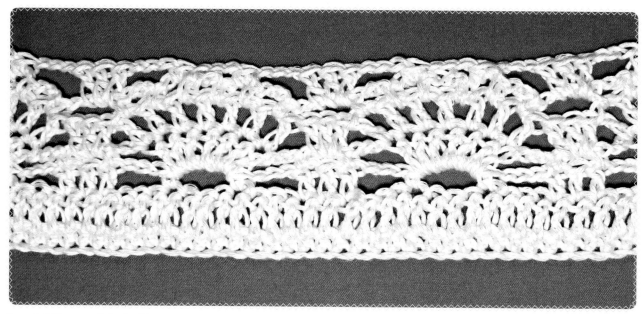

Step 5: What row 7 looks like

SLEEVES – Make 2

Row 1: Lay front and back pieces open and down flat, count to the right, counting down to the fourth shell from the shoulder, attach yarn and work 71sc across back, shoulder rows and front rows, over to fourth shell from the top on the front. Turn (this is the start of a sleeve).

Row 2: Ch3, 1dc in next sc, ch3, (skip next 3sc, 1sc in next sc, ch3) twice, *skip next 3sc, 1dc in next 3sc, ch3, (skip next 3sc, 1sc in next sc, ch3) twice* rep from * to * across to last 5sc, skip next 3sc, 1dc in last 2sc. Turn.

Row 3: Ch3, 1dc in next 2dc, ch3, skip next ch3 sp, 7dc in next ch3 sp, ch3, *skip next ch3 sp, 1sc in next dc, ch1, skip next dc, 1sc in next dc, ch3, skip next ch3 sp, 7dc in next ch3 sp, ch3* rep from * to * across to last ch3 sp, skip last ch3 sp, 1dc in last dc. Turn.

Row 4: Ch3, 1dc in next dc, ch3, skip next ch3 sp, 1dc in next dc, (ch1, 1dc in next dc) 6 times, *skip next ch3 sp, 3dc in next ch1 sp, skip next ch3 sp, 1dc in next dc, (ch1, 1dc in next dc) 6 times* rep from * to * across to last ch3 sp, skip last ch3 sp, ch3, 1dc in

Step 6: Sewing shoulder seams together

last 2dc. Turn.

Row 5: Ch3, 1dc in next dc, ch3, skip next ch3 sp, 1sc in next ch1 sp, (ch3, 1sc in next ch1 sp) 5 times, *ch3, skip next 5dc, 1sc in next ch1 sp, (ch3, 1sc in next ch1 sp) 5 times* rep from * to

* across to last 3dc, ch3, skip next dc, skip next ch3 sp, 1dc in last 2dc. Turn.

Row 6: Ch3, 1dc in next dc, ch3, skip next two ch3 sps, 1sc in next ch3 sp, ch3, skip next ch3 sp, 1sc in next ch3 sp, ch3, *skip next ch3 sp, 3dc in next

ch3 sp, ch3, (skip next ch3 sp, 1sc in next ch3 sp, ch3) twice* rep from * to * across to last 2sps, skip last 2sps, 2dc in third ch. Turn.

Rows 7–27: Repeat rows 3–6 in sequence.

Rows 28–30: Repeat rows 3–5 once. At end of row 30, fold sleeve in half and working in ends of row, sc tog the sleeve and then continue right down to the side of sweater and sc tog the sides. Fasten off and weave in ends.

SLEEVE TRIM

Round 1: Attach yarn to seam, ch1, sc in each ch3 sp around. Slst to join. (36sc)

Rounds 2–3: Ch1, 1sc in same st as joining, 1sc in each sc around. Slst to join. (36sc)

Round 4: Ch1, 1sc in same st as joining, skip next sc *5hdc in next sc, skip next sc, slst in next sc* rep from * to * around. Slst to join. Fasten off and weave in ends.

PLACETS

Note: Buttonholes are made on the right front side of cardigan.

Work rows 1–5 on each front of cardigan and across neck edge.

Row 1: Starting on bottom right side of cardigan, attach yarn, 1sc in each end of row up right side, across each st on neck edge and in each end of row down left front side. Turn.

Row 2: Ch1, 1sc in each sc on fronts and neck edge. Turn.

Row 3: Ch1, NOTE: you are going to make the buttonholes on this row. Work buttonholes evenly on right front stitches, making as many buttonholes as desired. To make a buttonhole: (ch2, skip next sc), working even amount of sc in between each buttonhole. Turn.

Row 4: Ch1, 1sc in each sc on each front and across neck edge. When you get to the buttonhole, just put one sc in each ch2 sp. Turn.

Row 5: Ch1, 1sc in next sc, skip next sc, 5hdc in next sc, skip next sc, slst in next sc, *5hdc in next sc, skip next sc, slst in next sc* rep from * to * across fronts and neck edge.

Do not turn, but now work across the bottom of the cardigan.

SCALLOPS FOR BOTTOM OF SWEATER

Row 1: 1sc in first st, *3sc in next ch3 sp, slst in next sc* rep from * to * across. At end of row fasten off and weave in ends.

Lacy Wrap

These beautiful lacy wraps can be made for anyone in the wedding party,

including the mother of the bride.

Materials

- Cascade Greenland, 100% Merino Superwash, 3.5oz/100g
  – Color name Turtle / Color # 3540 / 2 skeins
  –OR–
- Cascade 220 Superwash 100% Superwash Wool, #4 medium weight 100gr/220yds
  – Color name Orange / Color # 825 / 2 balls
- 1 button ⅝"
- Yarn needle

- **Hook:** US G/6 (4.00mm) Susan Bates

Skill level: Easy

Top edging measures 39" (44", 49") wide. Measurements include bust and arms. If you need a smaller or bigger wrap you can add or deduct multiple of 10sts. All wraps measure approx. 10" long. You can make wraps longer or shorter if desired by adding more rows or making fewer rows.

Glossary of abbreviations

ch – chain
dc – double crochet
hdc – half double crochet
rem – remaining
rep – repeat
*rep from * to * – repeat in between the stars
sc – single crochet
shell – 5hdc
sp – space
v-st – dc, ch2, dc, all in same st

Note: Ch3 counts as 1st dc

**SMALL, MEDIUM
AND LARGE WRAPS**
Instructions written for small, other sizes in parenthesis.

Start at top edge
Row 1: With G hook and Turtle or Orange, ch124, (134, 144) 1sc in second ch from hook, 1sc in each rem ch. Turn. (123sc, 133sc, 143sc)
Row 2: Ch3, 1dc in next 3sc, ch2, skip next 2sc, v-st in next sc, ch2, skip next 2sc, *1sc in next 5sc, ch2, skip next 2sc, v-st in next sc, ch2, skip next 2sc* rep from * to * across to last 4sc, 1dc

Step 1: Row 2

in each of the last 4sc. Turn.

Row 3: Ch3, 1dc in next 3dc, ch2, 7dc in next v-st, ch2, *skip next sc, 1sc in next 3sc, skip next sc, ch2, 7dc in next v-st, ch2* rep from * to * across to last 4dc, 1dc in last 4dc. Turn.

Row 4: Ch3, 1dc in next 3dc, ch2, (1dc, ch1) in next dc 6 times, 1dc in last dc, ch2 *skip next sc, 1sc in next sc, skip next sc, ch2, (1dc, ch1) in next dc, 6 times, 1dc in last dc, ch2* rep from * to * across to last 4dc, 1dc in last 4dc. Turn.

Row 5: Ch3, 1dc in next 3dc, ch3, skip ch2 and next dc, 1sc in next ch1sp, ch3, *1sc in next ch1sp, ch3* rep from * to * across, (making sure to work only in the ch1 spaces) work to last 4dc, 1dc in last 4dc. Turn.

Row 6: Ch3, 1dc in next 3dc, ch2, v-st in next ch3 sp, ch2, *skip next two ch3 sps, 5sc in next ch3 sp, ch2, skip next two ch3 sps, v-st in next ch3 sp, ch2* rep from * to * across to last 4dc, 1dc in last 4dc. Turn.

Row 7: Ch3, 1dc in next 3dc, ch2, 7dc in next v-st, ch2, *skip next sc, 1sc in next 3sc, skip next sc, ch2, 7dc in next v-st, ch2* rep from * to * across to last 4dc, 1dc in last 4dc. Turn.

Row 8: Ch3, 1dc in next 3dc, ch2, (1dc, ch1) in next dc 6 times, 1dc in last dc, ch2 *skip next sc, 1sc in next sc, skip next sc, ch2, (1dc, ch1) in next dc 6 times, 1dc in last dc, ch2* rep from * to * across to last 4dc, 1dc in last 4dc. Turn.

Row 9: Ch3, 1dc in next 3dc, ch3, skip ch2 and next dc, 1sc in next ch1 sp, ch3, *1sc in next ch1sp, ch3* rep from * to * across, (making sure to work only in the ch1 spaces) work to last 4dc, 1dc in last 4dc. Turn.

Rows 10–24: Repeat rows 6–9 in sequence 4 more times ending with row 8. At end of row 24 do not turn, but work up ends of rows to neck edge.

Step 2: Row 3

Step 3: Row 4

Step 4: Row 5

Step 5: Row 6

You now are going to work in around the outside of the wrap.

Round 1: Ch1, 2sc in each end of row up to top edge, 1sc in each st across top edging, 2sc in each end of row down left front, 1dc in next 4dc, ch3, skip ch2 and next dc, 1sc in next ch1 sp, ch3, *1sc in next ch1sp, ch3* rep from * to * across, (making sure to work only in the ch1 spaces) work to last 4dc, 1dc in last 4dc.
Slst to join round.
Round 2: Ch1, 1sc in same st as joining, skip next sc, *5hdc in next sc, skip next sc, slst in next sc, skip next sc* rep from * to * up right front, across top edge and down left front. Fasten off and weave in ends.

FLOWER

Round 1: With G hook and Turtle or Orange, ch2, 16sc in second ch from hook. Slst to join, ch1. (8sc)
Round 2: 1sc, 1hdc, 1dc, 1hdc, 1sc, all in same st as joining, slst in next sc, *(1sc, 1hdc, 1dc, 1hdc, 1sc) all in next sc, slst in next sc* rep from * to * around 6 more times to form 8 petals. Slst to join round. (8 petals)
Round 3: Ch3, push petals forward and sc in the back of the petals, between petals *ch3, sc between in back of petal* rep 6 more times. (8 ch3 loops made)
Round 4: 1sc, 1hdc, 3dc, 1hdc, 1sc in first ch3 loop, (1sc, 1hdc, 3dc, 1hdc, 1sc) in each ch3 loop around. (8 petals made)
Round 5: Ch4, push petals forward and sc in the back of the petals, between petals *ch4, sc between in back of petal* rep 6 more times. (8 ch4 loops made)
Round 6: 1sc, 1hdc, 5dc, 1hdc, 1sc in first ch4 loop, (1sc, 1hdc, 5dc, 1hdc, 1sc) in each ch4 loop around. (8 petals made) Fasten off and weave in ends.

FINISHING

Sew button to front of wrap. Push the button through any stitch on top of wrap. Put flower over button pushing through the center of the flower. Wrap can be adjusted by where you button the wrap.

Step 6: Round 3 of flower

Flowergirl Shrug

This easy-to-make shrug is a sweet accessory for the flowergirl.

Materials

- Kid Seta Noir, 60% Super Kid Mohair/22% silk/11% nylon/
  5% polyester/2%metallic, 25g/ .88oz/232yds/212m
  – Color name Berry / Color # 15 / 4 skeins

- **Hook:** US E/4 (3.50mm) Susan Bates

Skill level: Easy

Gauge: 9rows = 5", 2shells = 2"

Glossary of abbreviations

ch – chain
dc – double crochet
rep – repeat
*rep from * to * – repeat in between
  the stars
sc – single crochet
slst – slip stitch

Note: Instructions are written for 1–3yrs; 4–6yrs and 7–13yrs are in parenthesiss
Hold 2 strands of yarn throughout entire shrug

SHRUG

Row 1: Holding 2 strands of yarn together, ch46 (62, 69) 1sc in second ch from hook, 1sc in each remaining ch across. Ch1, turn. (45sc, 61sc, 68sc)

Row 2: 1dc in first sc, 1dc in next sc, skip next 3sc, (3dc, ch2, 1dc) all in next sc, *skip next 4sc, (3dc, ch2, 1dc) all in next sc* rep from * to * across to last 5sc, skip next 3sc, 1dc in last 2sc. Ch1, turn.

Row 3: 1dc in first 2dc, *(3dc, ch2, 1dc) all in next ch2 sp* repeat from * to * across, ending with 1dc in last 2dc. Ch1, turn.

Following rows: Repeat row 3 until shrug measures 25" (27", 33").

NEXT: 1sc in each st and end of rows around entire shrug. Slst to join round. Do not fasten off, but continue on to sleeves.

SLEEVES

Fold rows together the long way and work on the wrong side of shrug. Measure 5" on each end and sew together to form sleeves.

Turn to right side and attach yarn to end of sleeve opening.

NEXT: Work 5 rows of sc around each sleeve opening.

NEXT: *1slst in next sc, skip next sc, 5hdc in next sc, skip next sc* rep from * to * around sleeve opening. Slst to join round. Fasten off and weave in ends. Repeat for second sleeve trim.

FORMING COLLAR AND BOTTOM OF BACK

Ch2 counts as first dc.

Round 1: Attach yarn to any st near underarm, 1dc in first sc, 1dc in next sc, skip next 2sc, (3dc, ch2, 1dc) all in next sc, skip next 2sc, *(3dc, ch2, 1dc) all in next sc, skip next 2sc* rep from * to * around, 1dc in last 2sc. Slst to join round, ch2, turn.

Round 2: 1dc in first 2dc, *(3dc, ch2, 1dc) all in next ch2 sp* repeat from * to * across, ending with 1dc in the last dc. Ch2, turn.

Round 3: 1dc in next dc, *(3dc, ch2, 1dc) all in next ch2 sp* repeat from * to * across, ending with 1dc in each of the last 2dc. Ch2, turn.

Rounds 4–5: Repeat rounds 2–3.

Round 6: Ch1, 1sc in same st as joining, 1sc in next 2dc, *6dc in next ch2 sp, skip next 3dc, 1sc before next dc* repeat from * to * around. Fasten off, weave in ends.

Step 1: Row 2 of shrug

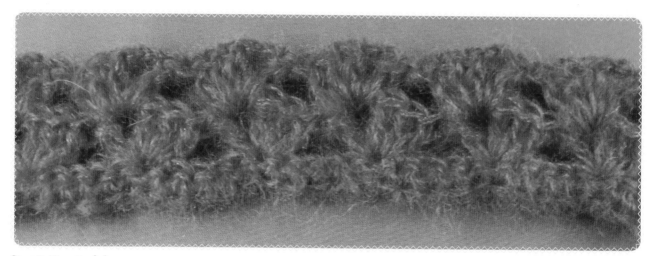

Step 2: Row 3 of shrug

Step 3: Sleeves for shrug

Step 4: Collar of shrug

Accessories

Flower Belt

Crochet Necklace

Wrist Corsage

Garter Belt

Ring Bearer Pillow

Flower Girl Basket Liner

Flower Belt

· ·

*Such a pretty accent — and easy to make — to wear with a white or off-white dress —
another way to add a dash of texture!*

Materials

· · · · · · · · · · · · · · · · ·

- Cascade Yarns Greenland, 100% merino superwash
  – Color name Turtle / Color # 3540 / 1 ball
- Cascade Sateen, 100% Acrylic, 100gr (3.5oz) 300.7 yards (275m)
  – Color name White / Color # 6 / 1 skein
- Yarn needle

- **Hook:** US G6 (5.00mm) Susan Bates

Skill level: Easy

Glossary of abbreviations

· ·

ch – chain
dc – double crochet
hdc – half double crochet
sc – single crochet
prev – previous
yo – yarn over
dc cluster – to make a dc cluster,
ch3, yo, insert hook in between
prev dc cluster, bring yarn back
through, yo, drop off first 2 loops,
yo, insert hook in between prev
dc cluster in same spot, bring yarn
back through, yo, drop off first 2
loops, yo, drop off last 3 loops.

BELT

Row 1: Ch3, 2dc cluster in third ch
from hook.
Row 2: Ch3, 2dc cluster in between 2
sts of dc cluster.
Repeat row 2 until belt goes around
child and ties in a nice bow in the back.

ROSES

First rose: Ch13, 3sc in second ch from
hook, 3sc in next 3ch, 3hdc in next
4ch, 3dc in next 4ch. Roll stitches into
a rose shape, ch1, 1sc in rolled stitches
to hold stitches into a rose shape.
Do not fasten off but continue on to
next rose.
All roses: Repeat same as for first rose
to make a garland of roses approx.
20" long. Fasten off leaving a tail to sew
with. Sew roses to front middle of belt.

Step 1: Where to insert hook for dc cluster

Step 2: Last 3 loops on hook

Step 3: Drop off all 3 loops (completed dc cluster)

Step 4: Roll stitches into a flower

Step 5: Sc together all the layers of the rose to hold rose shape

Step 6: Finished 2nd flower

Crochet Necklace

Adding meaningful personal embellishments can make this wedding day adornment a one-of-a-kind accessory.

Materials

- Cascade Heritage Silk, 85% MerinoSuperwash Wool/15% Mulberry Silk, 100gr (3.5 oz) / 437yds (400 m)
  – Color name Ivory / Color # 5618 / 2 skeins
- Decorative Buttons
- Yarn needle

- **Hook:** US D/3 (3.25mm) Susan Bates

Skill level: Easy

Measurement: Necklace measures 15" long

Glossary of abbreviations

ch – chain
dc – double crochet
hdc – half double crochet
rem – remaining
rep – repeat
*rep from * to * – repeat in between the stars
sc – single crochet
slst – slip stitch
sp – space
st – stitch
trc – treble crochet

NECKLACE
Row 1: Ch3, 1dc in third ch from hook. Do not turn.
Row 2: Ch3, 1dc in between first ch3 and dc. Do not turn.
Repeat row 2 until necklace is approx. 48" long. Slst to row 1 to make a large circle, fasten off and weave in ends. Wrap necklace around neck 4 times. Take off neck and put aside for now.

LARGE LEAF – Make one
Round 1: Ch2, 12sc in second ch from hook. (12sc)
Round 2: 2sc in next sc, 2hdc in next 2sc, 2dc in next 2sc, 3trc in next sc, 2dc in next 2sc, 2hdc in next 2sc, 2sc in next 2sc.
Round 3: 1sc in next 7sts, 1hdc in next st, 1dc in next 2sts, 1trc in next st, 3trc in next st, 1trc in next st, 1dc in next 2sts, 1hdc in next st, 1sc in next 9sc.

Step 1: large leaf (L1)

Round 4: (1slst, ch1) in next 13sts, ch4, 1slst in next st, (1slst, ch1) in each rem st. Fasten off leaving a tail to sew with.

MEDIUM LEAF – Make one
Round 1: Ch2, 12sc in second ch from hook. (12sc)
Round 2: 2sc in next sc, 2hdc in next 2sc, 2dc in next 2sc, 3trc in next sc, 2dc in next 2sc, 2hdc in next 2sc, 2sc in next 2sc.
Round 3: (1slst, ch1) in next 8sts, ch4, 1slst in next st, (1slst, ch1) in each rem st. Fasten off leaving a tail to sew with.

SMALL LEAF – Make 2
Round 1: Ch2, 7sc in second ch from hook. (7sc)
Round 2: 2sc in next sc, 2hdc in next sc, 2dc in next sc, 3trc in next sc, 2dc in next sc, **2hdc** in next sc, 2sc in next sc.
Round 3: (1slst, ch1) in next 5sts, ch4, 1slst in next st, (1slst, ch1) in each rem st. Fasten off leaving a tail to sew with.

LARGE FLOWER
Note: This flower has 3 layers
First layer
Round 1: Ch2, 6sc in second ch from hook. Work in continuous rounds. (6sc)
Round 2: 2sc in each sc around. (12sc)
Round 3: *1sc in next sc, 2sc in next sc* rep from * to * around. (18sc)
Round 4: *1sc in next 2sc, 2sc in next sc* rep from * to * around. (24sc)
Round 5: *1sc in next 3sc, 2sc in next sc* rep from * to * around. (30sc)
Round 6: 1slst in next sc, 5hdc in next sc, *skip next sc, 1slst in next sc, 5hdc in next sc* rep from * to * around. Slst to join round, fasten off leaving a tail to sew with.

Second layer
Rounds 1–4: repeat rounds 1–4 of first layer.
Round 5: (1slst, ch1) in each sc around. Slst to join round, fasten off leaving a tail to sew with.

Step 2: Medium leaf (L2)

Step 3: Small Leaf (L3)

Step 4: The 3 parts of the large flower

Step 5: Put layers together (F1)

Third layer

Rounds 1–2: repeat rounds 1–2 same as first layer.

Round 3: (1slst, ch1) in each sc around. Slst to join round, fasten off, leaving a tail to sew with. Sew all layers together as shown in picture and sew decorative button in center of flower.

IRISH ROSE

Round 1: Ch2, 6sc in second ch from hook. Slst to join. (6sc)

Round 2: (Sc, hdc, dc, hdc, sc) all in same st as joining, (sc, hdc, dc, hdc, sc) in each sc around, to form 6 petals. Slst to join.

Round 3: Holding petals forward, *ch3, working in the back of the petals, sc in between the petals* repeat from * to * 5 more times.

Round 4: (Sc, hdc, 3dc, hdc, sc) work all these stitches in each of the ch3 loops. Slst to join.

Round 5: Repeat round 3.

Round 6: (Sc, hdc, 5dc, hdc, sc) work all these stitches in each of the ch3 loops. Slst to join.

Fasten off leaving a tail to sew with. Add embellishments to flower if desired.

FLOWER

Round 1: Ch2, 12sc in second ch from hook. (12sc)

Round 2: 1sc in next sc, *ch6, skip next sc, 1sc in next sc* rep from * to * around. (6 petals started.)

Round 3: *(1sc, 1hdc, 3dc, 1hdc, 1sc) all in ch6 sp* rep from * to * in each ch6 sp. Slst to join round, fasten off leaving a tail to sew with. Sew on decorative button.

NEXT: Sew leaves and flowers onto strands as shown in step by steps. Or arrange them in your own desired positions. I found it easier to sew the flowers and leaves together first, and then sew them onto the necklace as a whole.

Step 6: Irish rose (F2)

Step 7: Flower (F3)

Step 8: Position of flowers of necklace in pictures

Step 9: Flowers sewn together with embellishments

Wrist Corsage

This quick, easy and fun wrist corsage can be made not only for the bride,
but for the whole wedding party.

Materials

- Prism Yarn – Wild Stuff Half Hank Yarn, 150yds (4oz), Fiber: Rayon, Cotton, Nylon, Kid Mohair, Bamboo, Tencel Wool, Alpaca, Poly – Color name Antique / 1 skein
- ½" elastic cord – 7½" long
- 1 decorative button
- A few beads
- Fabric glue
- Yarn needle

- **Hook:** US K/10.5 (6.50mm) Susan Bates

Skill level: Easy

Flower measures approx. 4" across

Glossary of abbreviations

ch – chain
dc – double crochet
hdc – half double crochet
rep – repeat
*rep from * to * – repeat in between
   the stars
sc – single crochet
slst – slip stitch

WRIST BAND

Cut a length of elastic cord approx. 7½" long. Overlap ends approx. ½" and sew ends tog.
Round 1: With Antique and K hook, sc around cord, working as many sc as needed to go around entire band. Slst to join. ch1.
Round 2: Now working over the stitches from round 1. Work sc around entire band until round 1 is covered. Slst to join. Fasten off and weave in ends.

FLOWER

Round 1: With antique and K hook, ch 2, 6sc in second ch from hook. Slst to join. (6sc)
Round 2: (Sc, hdc, dc, hdc, sc) all in same st as joining, (sc, hdc, dc, hdc, sc) in each sc around, to form 6 petals. Slst to join.
Round 3: Holding petals forward,

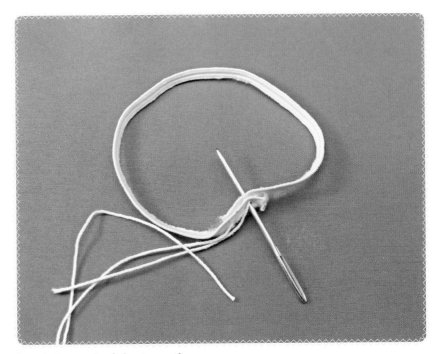

Step 1: Sew ends of elastic together

ch3, working in the back of the petals, sc in between the petals repeat around 5 more times.

Round 4: (Sc, hdc, 3dc, hdc, sc) work all these stitches in each of the ch3 loops. Slst to join.

Round 5: Repeat round 3.

Round 6: (Sc, hdc, 5dc, hdc, sc) work all these stitches in each of the ch3 loops. Slst to join.

Fasten off leaving a tail to sew with. Add embellishments to flower if desired. Sew flower onto wrist band. Weave in all ends.

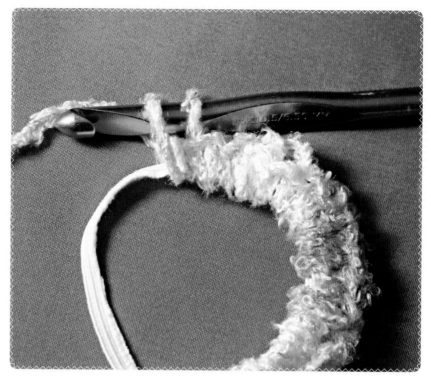

Step 2: Sc around cord

Step 3: Working over the first row of sc

Step 4: Making the loops behind the flower

Garter Belt

A garter belt is a must-have for your wedding day, why not make your own?

Materials

- Aunt Lydia's Size 10 Crochet Cotton, 500yds
  – Color name White / 1 ball
- ⅜" elastic cord: 20–22" length
- Embellishments to decorate flower center and leaves
- Craft glue
- Tapestry needle

- **Hook:** Steel hook size US 8 (1.25mm)

Skill level: Easy

Glossary of abbreviations

ch – chain
dc – double crochet
hdc – half double crochet
rem – remaining
rep – repeat
*rep from * to * – repeat in between the stars
sc – single crochet
slst – slip stitch
trc – treble crochet

Note: Picot – ch3, slst in top of fourth dc

GARTER

Cut a length of elastic cord to desired width to fit thigh. Most women's thighs are approx. 20–22", so cut elastic about an inch smaller than desired.
Take elastic cord and overlap ends about ½" and sew together.
Round 1: With White and size 8 steel hook and elastic cord, working over the cord, work sc evenly around entire cord until the cord is covered with sc. Slst to join.
Round 2: Working in back loop of sc only, ch1, 1sc in same st as joining, *skip next 3sc, (4dc, picot, 3dc all in next sc) skip next 3sc, 1sc in next sc* rep from * to * around. Slst to join.
Round 3: Ch1, turn garter so that scallops are facing right way up, pull the tips towards you, and working on opposite side of round 2, 1sc in unworked loop on opposite side of first sc, *skip next 3 unworked loops, (4dc, picot, 3dc all in next unworked loop) skip next 3 unworked loops, 1sc

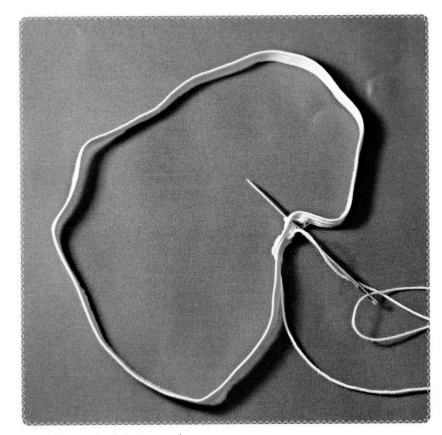

Step 1: Sew ends of elastic together

in next unworked loop *rep from * to* around. Slst to join. Fasten off and weave in ends.

LARGE FLOWER – Make 1

Round 1: With White and size 8 steel hook, ch 2, 6sc in second ch from hook. Slst to join. (6sc)

Round 2: (Sc, hdc, dc, hdc, sc) all in same st as joining, (sc, hdc, dc, hdc, sc) in each sc around, to form 6 petals. Slst to join.

Round 3: Holding petals forward, *ch3, working in the back of the petals, sc around the post that is visible between the petals* repeat around 5 more times.

Round 4: (Sc, hdc, 3dc, hdc, sc) work all these stitches in each of the ch3 loops. Slst to join.

Round 5: Repeat round 3.

Round 6: (sc, hdc, 5dc, hdc, sc) work all these stitches in each of the ch3 loops. Slst to join.

Round 7: Repeat round 3.

Round 8: (Sc, hdc, 7dc, hdc, sc) work all these stitches in each of the ch3 loops. Slst to join

Round 9: Holding petals forward, *ch4, working in the back of the petals, sc around the post that is visible between the petals* repeat around 5 more times.

Round 10: (sc, hdc, 9dc, hdc, sc) work all these stitches in each of the ch4 loops. Slst to join.

Round 11: Repeat round 9.

Round 12: (Sc, hdc, 11dc, hdc, sc) work all these stitches in each of the ch4 loops. Slst to join. Do not fasten off but continue on to stems.

STEMS

Note: The stem is just a row of sc that is sewn on top of scallops. Your leaves are then sewn on top of stems.

With size 8 steel hook, ch41, 1sc in second ch from hook, 1sc in each rem ch. Slst to flower, ch10, skip next 3 petals, slst in between next 2 petals,

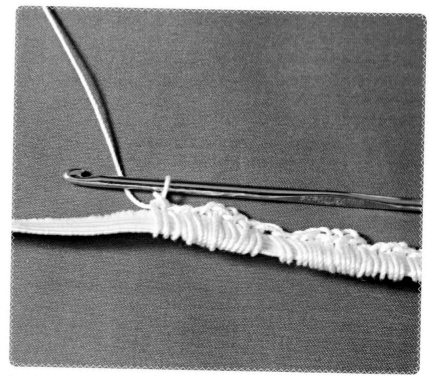

Step 2: Sc around cord

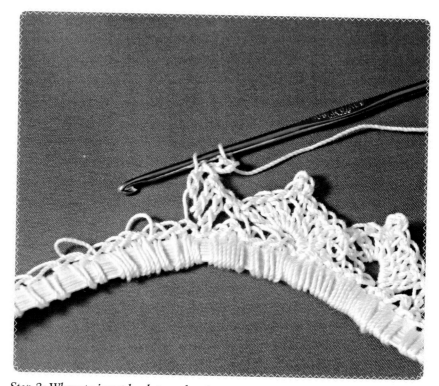

Step 3: Where to insert hook to make picot

ch41, 1sc in second ch from hook, 1sc in each rem ch, slst to flower. Fasten off leaving a tail to sew with. Sew flower and stems onto garter.

LEAVES – Make 8
With White and size 8 steel hook , ch8, 1sc in second ch from hook, 1hdc in next ch, 1dc in next ch, 1trc in next ch, 1dc in next ch, 1hdc in next ch, 2sc in last ch. Now working on opposite side of ch, 1hdc in next ch, 1dc in next ch, 1trc in next ch, 1dc in next ch, 1hdc in next ch, 1sc in next ch, slst to join. Fasten off leaving a tail to sew with. Sew 4 leaves on each side of flower.

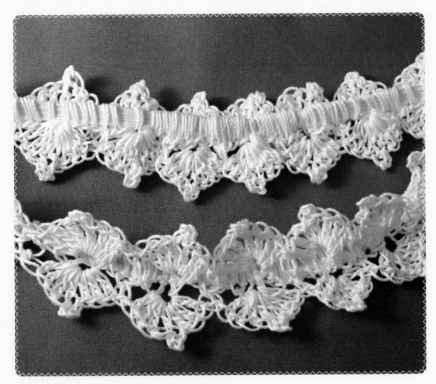

Step 4: Working on other side of garter

Step 5: Sewing stem on elastic

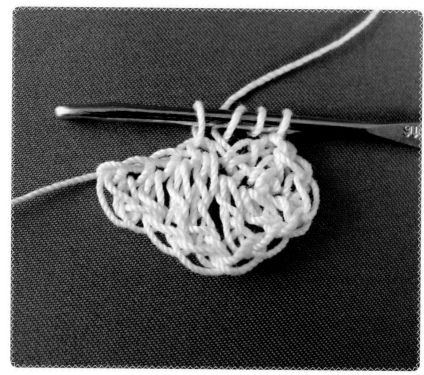

Step 6: Working on back side of leaf

Step 7: Embellish large flower with bead

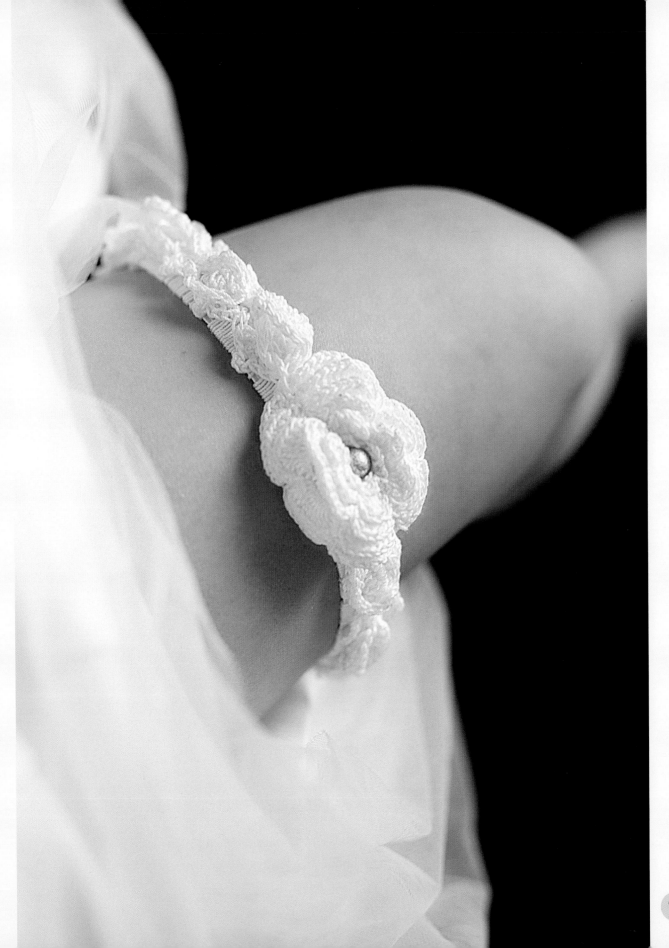

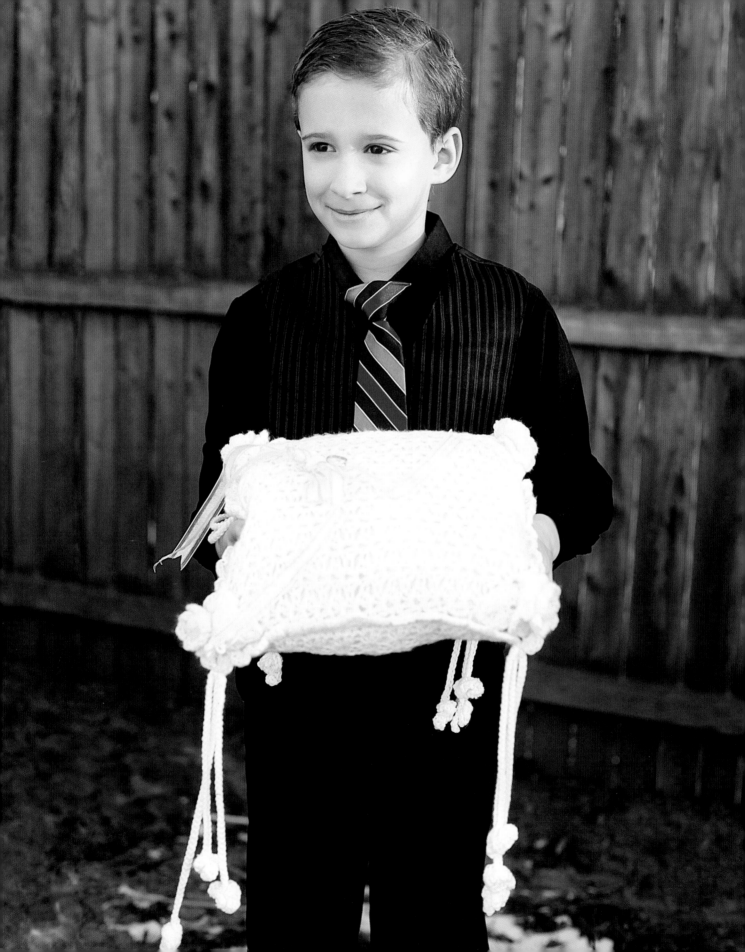

Ring Bearer Pillow

Cascading flowers of hooked yarn adorn this lovely ring bearer pillow.

Materials

- Cascade Sateen, 100% acrylic, 300.7yds/275m/100g/3.5oz
  – Color name White / Color # 6 / 2 skeins
- Pillow form 12" x 12"
- 24" ribbon
- Yarn needle

- **Hook:** US E/4 (3.50mm) Susan Bates

Skill level: Easy

Glossary of abbreviations

ch – chain
dc – double crochet
rem – remaining
rep – repeat
*rep from * to * – repeat in between
   the stars
sc – single crochet
slst – slip stitch

PILLOW COVER

Row 1: Ch37, 1dc in fourth ch from hook, ch2, 1sc in same ch, *skip next 2ch, (2dc, ch2, 1sc) in next ch* rep from * to * across. Turn.

Row 2: Ch3, 1dc in next ch2 sp, ch2, 1sc in same ch2 sp, (2dc, ch2, 1sc) in each ch2 sp across. Turn.

Rep row 2 until work measures 12".

Round 1: Work 1sc in each end of row and each st around all four sides, working stitches evenly. Slst to first st to join round. Fasten off.

NEXT: Hold wrong sides together, sc together both side, working three sides and then insert pillow form, continue to sc together the fourth side. Slst to join round together.

Scallop Round: 1sc in same st as joining, (*5dc in next sc, slst in next sc* rep from * to * to first corner, ch41, 1slst in second ch from hook, 1slst in each rem ch, slst into same st as beg, ch51, 1slst in second ch from hook, 1slst in each rem ch, slst into same st as beg, ch46, 1slst in second ch from hook, 1slst in each rem ch, 1slst in same st as beg.) Rep from (to) 3 more times. Fasten off and weave in ends.

Step 1: Row 1 of pillow cover

SMALL HANGING FLOWERS – Make 12

Ch10, 2sc in second ch from hook, 2sc in next 2ch, 2hdc in next 3ch, 2dc in next 3ch, (leaf) ch6, 1sc in second ch from hook, 1hdc in next ch, 1dc in next ch, 1hdc in next ch, 1sc in next ch. Fasten off leaving tail to sew with. Roll stitches into a flower, leaving leaf off to side. Run a stitch through bottom of the rows to hold the rose together. Sew small roses to bottom of each ch in each corner of pillow.

LARGE CORNER FLOWER – Make 4

Row 1: Ch14, 2dc in third ch from hook, 3dc in each rem ch, ch1 turn. (36dc)

Row 2: 1slst in each dc across, ch1, turn. (36slst)

Row 3: (1slst underneath next slst, 1hdc, 1dc, 1hdc all underneath next slst) repeat 2 more times. (1slst underneath next slst, 1hdc, 2dc, 1hdc all underneath next slst) repeat 2 more times. (1slst underneath next slst, 1hdc, 3dc, 1hdc all underneath next slst) repeat 2 more times. (1slst underneath next slst, 1hdc, 4dc, 1hdc all underneath next slst) repeat 2 more times. (1slst underneath next slst, 1hdc, 5dc, 1hdc all underneath next slst) repeat 2 more times. (1slst underneath next slst, 1hdc, 6dc, 1hdc all underneath next slst) repeat 1 more time. Fasten off, leaving a long tail to sew with.

Roll stitches into a flower, and run a stitch along bottom to connect all rows. Put aside for now.

Step 2: Row 2 of pillow cover

Step 3: How the pattern looks when worked up

LARGE LEAF – Make 8

Round 1: Ch2, 8sc in second ch from hook, slst to join, ch1.

Round 2: 2sc in same st as joining, 2hdc in next sc, 2dc in next sc, 3trc in next sc, ch3, slst in top of last trc, 2trc in same sc, 2dc in next sc, 2sc in next 2sc, slst to join, fasten off, leaving a tail to sew with.

Sew 2 leaves in back of large flower. Sew flower to corner of pillow.

Step 4: Scallop round

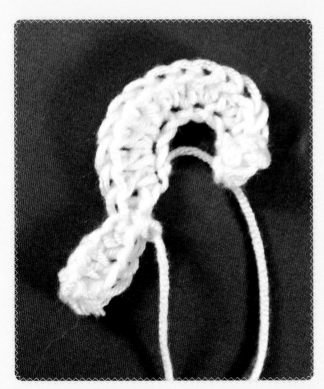

Step 5: Small flower unrolled

Step 6: Small flower rolled

Step 7: Unrolled large flower

Step 8: Large flower rolled

Step 9: Run a stitch along bottom of flower to connect

Step 10: Large leaf

FINISHING

Hold two ribbons together. Cut ribbons to desired lengths. Push ribbons under a couple of stitches in middle of pillow and tie into a knot. Place wedding rings on ribbons. Tie ribbons into a bow.

Flower Girl Basket Liner

A fun way to add a personal touch to the flower girl basket, the liner will transform an ordinary basket into something special and remain a treasured heirloom doily.

Materials

- Cascade Sateen, 100% acrylic, 300.7yds/275m/100g/3.5oz
  - Color name White / Color # 6 / 1 skein
  - Color name Sand / Color # 22 / 1 skein
- Red Heart Super Soft, 100% acrylic, 515 yds/471m/ 283g/10 oz
  - Color name Dark Leaf / Color # 9523 / 2ounces needed of the Dark Leaf to make the leaves
- Yarn needle

- **Hook:** US F/5 (3.75mm) Susan Bates

Skill level: Easy

Basket: Top diameter: 9", depth: 4", Bottom diameter: 7"
Doily diameter: 34" circumference

Glossary of abbreviations

ch – chain
dc – double crochet
hdc – half double crochet
rep – repeat
*rep from * to * – repeat in between the stars
sc – single crochet
slst – slip stitch
st – stitch

Note: Ch3 counts as first dc.

BASKET LINING / DOILY
Round 1: With F hook and White, ch3, 11dc in third ch from hook. Slst to join. (12dc)
Round 2: Ch3, 1dc in same st as joining, 2dc in each dc around. Slst to join. (24dc)
Round 3: Ch3, 2dc in next dc, *1dc in next dc, 2dc in next dc* rep from * to * around. Slst to join. (36dc)
Round 4: Ch3, 1dc in next dc, 2dc in next dc, *1dc in next 2dc, 2dc in next dc* rep from * to * around. Slst to join. (48dc)
Round 5: Ch3, 1dc in next 2dc, 2dc in next dc, *1dc in next 3dc, 2dc in next dc* rep from * to * around. Slst to

join. (60dc)
Round 6: Ch3, 1dc in next 3dc, 2dc in next dc, *1dc in next 4dc, 2dc in next dc* rep from * to * around. Slst to join. (72dc)
Round 7: Ch3, 1dc in each dc around. Slst to join. (72dc)
Round 8: Ch3, 1dc in next 4dc, 2dc in next dc, *1dc in next 5dc, 2dc in next dc* rep from * to * around. Slst to join. (84dc)
Round 9: Ch3, 1dc in each dc around. Slst to join. (84dc)
Round 10: Ch3, 1dc in next 5dc, 2dc in next dc, *1dc in next 6dc, 2dc in next dc* rep from * to * around. Slst to join. (96dc)
Round 11: Ch3, 1dc in each dc around. Slst to join. (96dc)

Round 12: Ch3, 1dc in next 6dc, 2dc in next dc, *1dc in next 7dc, 2dc in next dc* rep from * to * around. Slst to join. (108dc)
Round 13: Ch3, 1dc in each dc around. Slst to join. (108dc)
Round 14: Ch3, 1dc in next 7dc, 2dc in next dc, *1dc in next 8dc, 2dc in next dc* rep from * to * around. Slst to join. (120dc)
Round 15: Ch1, 1sc in same st as joining, 1sc in next 7dc, skip next dc, 9dc in next dc, *skip next dc, 1sc in next 7dc, skip next dc, 9dc in next dc* rep from * to * around. Skip first sc, slst to join round in next sc.
Round 16: Ch1, skip same st as joining, *1sc in next 5sc, skip next sc, 1dc in next 4dc, 3dc in next dc, 1dc in

next 4dc, skip next sc* rep from * to * around. Skip first sc, slst to join round in next sc.

Round 17: Ch1, 1sc in same st as joining, *1sc in next 3sc, skip next sc, 1dc in next 4dc, 2dc in next dc, 3dc in next dc, 2dc in next dc, 1dc in next 4dc, skip next sc* rep from * to * around. Slst to join.

Round 18: Ch1, 1sc in next sc, skip next sc, (1dc, ch1) 14 times, 1dc in next dc, *skip next sc, 1sc in next sc, skip next sc, (1dc, ch1) 14 times, 1dc in next dc* rep from * to* around. Slst to join.

Round 19: Ch1, 1sc in same st as joining, (ch3, 1sc in next ch1 sp) rep around working in only the ch1 spaces. Slst to join. Fasten off and weave in ends.

LEAVES – Make 12

Round 1: With Dark Leaf, ch7, 1sc in second ch from hook, 1hdc in next ch, 1dc in next ch, 1hdc in next ch, 2sc in last ch, ch3, slst in top of last sc, 1sc in same last ch. Now working on opposite side of ch, 1hdc in next ch, 1dc in next ch, 1hdc in next ch, 1sc in last ch. Slst to join round. Fasten off leaving a tail to sew with. Put aside for now.

Step 1:Round 15

Step 2: Round 16

Step 3: Round 17

Step 4: Round 18

FLOWERS – Make 12

Row 1: With Sand, ch24, 1dc in sixth ch from hook, *ch2, skip next 2ch, 1dc in next ch* rep from * to * across. Ch1, turn.

Row 2: 1sc in dc, 5dc in next ch2 sp, 1sc in next dc, 5dc in next ch2 sp, (1sc in next dc, 7dc in next ch2 sp,) rep once more, (1sc in next dc, 9dc in next ch2 sp) rep once more, 1sc in next dc, 11dc in last ch2sp. Fasten off leaving a tail to sew with. Roll stitches into a rose, thread yarn needle and run a few stitches through the bottom of the flower to hold it together. Sew leaf to back side of flower. Sew flowers to each scallop.

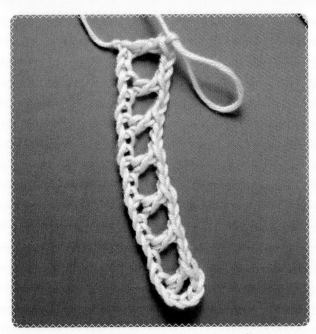

Step 5: Row 1 Flower

Step 6: Flower unrolled

Step 7: Flower rolled

Step 8: Working on opposite side of chain

Table Decorations

Wedding Cake Favors

Candy Bowl Wedding Favors

Wedding Cake Favors

These fun mini wedding cake favors are quick and easy!

Materials

- Cascade Sateen, 100% acrylic, 300.7yds/275m/100g/3.5oz
  – Color name White / Color # 6 / 1 skein
- Strands of crafting pearls
- Ribbon roses, satin roses or desired embellishments
- Yarn needle
- 3 cotton balls

- **Hook:** US D/3 (3.25mm) Susan Bates

Skill level: Easy

Cake measurements: Plate is 3" wide, Favor is 3" tall when put together.

Glossary of abbreviations

ch – chain
hdc – half double crochet
*rep from * to * – repeat in between the stars
sc – single crochet
slst– slip stitch
sp – space
tog – together

CAKE

Bottom Layer

Round 1: Ch2, 6sc in second ch from hook. Work in continuous spiral. (6sc)
Round 2: 2sc in each sc around. (12sc)
Round 3: 2sc in each sc around. (24sc)
Round 4: *1sc in next 3sc, 2sc in next sc* rep from * to * around. (30sc)
Round 5: 1sc in the back loop of each sc around. (30sc)
Round 6: 1sc in each sc around. (30sc)
Round 7: *1sc in next 3sc, sc tog the next 2sc* rep from * to * around. (24sc)
Round 8: 1sc in each sc around. (24sc)
Fasten off leaving a tail to sew with.

Middle Layer

Round 1: Ch2, 6sc in second ch from hook. Work in continuous spiral. (6sc)
Round 2: 2sc in each sc around. (12sc)
Round 3: 2sc in each sc around. (24sc)

Step 1: Bottom layer

Step 2: Middle layer

Step 3: Top layer

Round 4: 1sc in the back loop of each sc around. (24sc)
Round 5: *1sc in next 2sc, sc tog the next 2sc* rep from * to * around. (18sc)
Round 6: 1sc in each sc around. (18sc)
Fasten off leaving a tail to sew with.

Top Layer
Round 1: Ch2, 6sc in second ch from hook. Work in continuous spiral. (6sc)
Round 2: 2sc in each sc around. (12sc)
Round 3: 1sc in the back loop of each sc around. (12sc)
Round 4: 1sc in each sc around. (12sc)
Fasten off leaving a tail to sew with.

CAKE PLATE
Round 1: Ch2, 6sc in second ch from hook. Work in continuous spiral. (6sc)
Round 2: 2sc in each sc around. (12sc)
Round 3: 2sc in each sc around. (24sc)
Round 4: *1sc in next 3sc, 2sc in next sc* rep from * to * around. (30sc)

Step 4: Cake plate

Round 5: 1sc in each sc around. (30sc)
Round 6: 1slst in next sc, skip next sc, *5hdc in next sc, skip next sc, 1slst in next sc* rep from * to * around. Fasten off leaving a tail to sew with.

ASSEMBLY
Take top layer and put cotton ball inside it. Sew top lay to middle layer, sewing round 4 of top layer to round 5 of middle layer. Then put cotton ball in middle layer and sew middle layer to bottom layer. Then put 2 or 3 cotton balls in bottom layer and sew cake plate to bottom layer. Decorate with pearls, ribbons and other embellishments as desired.

Step 5: Stuff layers with cotton balls

Step 6: Sew together

Candy Bowl Wedding Favors

Here's a memorable wedding favor; fill it with candy or potpourri

and embellish with ribbons, fun buttons, or rosettes.

Materials

- Aunt Lydia's Fashion 3 Cotton , 150yds
  – Color name White / 1 ball
- Tapestry needle
- Aileen's Fabric Stiffener or 2 parts Elmer's glue to 1part water
- Tulle
- ⅛" ribbon
- Small flowers
- 3" round balls
- Wax paper
- Plastic wrap

- **Hook:** US D/3 (3.25mm) Susan Bates

Skill level: Easy

Measurements: Bowl = 3½" wide,
Plate = 4" wide

Glossary of abbreviations

ch – chain
dc – double crochet
rep – repeat
*rep from * to * – repeat in between
   the stars
sc – single crochet
tog – together

BOWL
Round 1: Ch2, 6sc in second ch from hook. Work in continuous rounds. (6sc)
Round 2: 2sc in each sc around. (12sc)
Round 3: *1sc in next sc, 2sc in next sc* rep from * to * around. (18sc)
Round 4: *1sc in next 2sc, 2sc in next sc* rep from * to * around. (24sc)
Round 5: *1sc in next 3sc, 2sc in next sc* rep from * to * around. (30sc)

Rounds 6–10: 1sc in each sc around. (30sc)
Round 11: *1sc in next 3sc, sc tog the next 2sc* rep from * to * around. (24sc)
Round 12: 1sc in each sc around. (24sc)
Round 13: *1slst in next sc, 6dc in next sc, skip next sc* rep from * to * around. (8 scallops) Fasten off and weave in ends.

BASE
Rounds 1–5: Repeat rounds 1–5 of bowl. (30sc)
Round 6: 1sc in each sc around. (30sc)
Round 7: *1slst in next sc, skip next sc, 6dc in next sc, skip next sc* rep from * to * around. (7 scallops)
Fasten off and weave in ends.

HOW TO STIFFEN BOWL AND BASE:

1. First put down enough wax paper to hold all of your favors.

2. Cover 3" ball with plastic wrap.

3. Put some fabric stiffener in a container.

4. Place bowls and bases into container.

5. Squeeze glue through all the pieces that you want stiffened, getting them all totally saturated.

6. Squeeze excess glue out of pieces and place bowls around 3" balls to stiffen and place bases on wax paper and press flat.

7. Place another piece of wax paper over bases and put something onto top of bases so that they will dry flat.

8. Let pieces dry for about 24 hours. After they are dry, glue base to bowl.

9. Place some tulle inside of bowl.

10. Put some potpourri or candy into the bowls.

11. Add desired embellishments such as ribbons and small flowers to decorate favors.

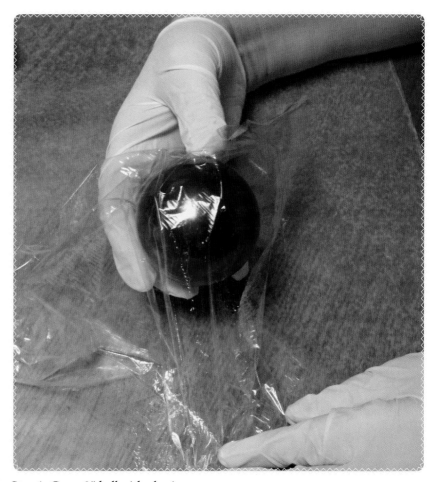

Step 1: Cover 3" ball with plastic wrap

Step 2: Place bowls and bases into container

Step 3: Squeeze glue through all the pieces to be stiffened, getting them all totally saturated

Step 4: Place bowls around 3" balls to stiffen

Step 5: Place bases on wax paper and press flat

Gloves and Purses

Above-the-Elbow Fingerless Wedding Gloves

The classic above-the-elbow gloves get a new twist with Irish roses at the cuff and an elegant crochet pattern — they're sure to become an heirloom.

Materials

- Aunt Lydia's Fashion 3 Crochet Cotton, 150yds
  – Color name White / 5 balls
- ⅛" elastic cord – 18" long x 2
- Decorative buttons
- Decorative pearl
- Yarn needle

- **Hook:** US D/3 (3.25mm) Susan Bates

Skill level: Easy

Gauge: 2 rows – 1",
1 shell and 1 v-st – 1"

Glossary of abbreviations

ch – chain
dc – double crochet
hdc – half double crochet
rem – remaining
rep – repeat
*rep from * to * – repeat in between
   the stars
sc – single crochet
shell – 5dc in ch 2 space
slst – slip stitch
trc – treble crochet
v-st – 1dc, ch2, 1dc all in same stitch

LONG FINGERLESS GLOVES

Starting at finger tips end.
Round 1: Ch42, slst to first ch to form a circle, ch1, 1sc in same st as joining, 1sc in each rem ch around. Slst to join. (42sc)
Round 2: Ch3, 4dc in same st as joining, skip next 2sc, v-st in next sc *skip next 2sc, 5dc in next sc, skip next 2sc, v-st in next sc* rep from * to * around. Slst to join in top of ch3.
Round 3: Make 2 slst to reach the third dc of the shell below, ch5, 1dc in same st as joining, shell in next v-st space, *v-st in middle dc of next shell, shell in next v-st space* rep from * to * around. Slst to third ch to join.
Round 4: Slst into ch2 sp, ch3, 4dc in

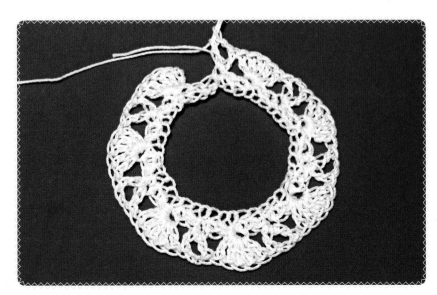

Step 1: Round 2

same ch2 sp, v-st in middle dc of next shell, *shell in next v-st space, v-st in middle dc of next shell* rep from * to * around. Slst to top of ch3.

Rounds 5–42: Repeat rounds 3 and 4 alternately until desired length of gloves.

Round 43: Ch1, 1sc in same st as joining, skip next dc, 1sc in next dc, skip next dc, 1sc in next 2dc, 1sc in next ch2 sp, *1sc in next 2dc, skip next dc, 1sc in next dc, skip next dc, 1sc in next 2dc, 1sc in next ch2sp* rep from * to * around, slst to join. (42st) Do not fasten off, but continue on to upper arm cuff.

UPPER ARM CUFF

Cut a piece of elastic cord that will fit comfortably around upper arm. Overlap 1" and sew ends together to form a circle.

Round 1: ch1, hold elastic inside glove and insert hook in joining sc from round 43, bring yarn back through, yo around elastic, drop off 2 loops. Continue joining elastic to top of glove with 1sc in each sc around. Slst to join, ch1. (See steps 4, 5, and 6) (42sc)

Round 2: 1sc in same st as joining, 1sc in each sc around. Slst to join, ch1, turn. (42sc)

Round 3: 1sc in BL of same st as joining, 1sc in the BL of each sc around. Slst to join, ch1. (42sc)

Rounds 4–8: 1sc in each sc around, slst to join, ch1. (42sc)

Round 9: 1sc in same st as joining, ch3, sc in same st, *1sc in each of the next 3sc, ch3, sc in same sc* repeat from * to * around to make picots. Slst to join. Fasten off and tie in ends.

Step 2: Round 3

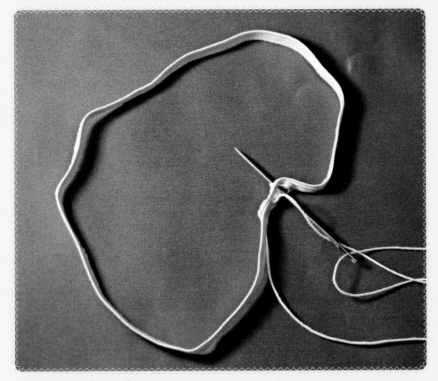

Step 3: Sew ends together

Step 4: Work sc around elastic

FINGER PICOTS

Round 1: Attach yarn to opposite side of starting ch, 1sc in same st as joining, ch3, sc same st, *1sc in each of the next 3sc, ch3, sc in same sc* repeat from * to * around to make picots. Slst to join, fasten off and weave in ends. Repeat for other glove.

BASIC IRISH ROSE

Round 1: With White and D hook, ch 2, 6sc in second ch from hook. Slst to join. (6sc)

Round 2: (Sc, hdc, dc, hdc, sc) work all these stitches in each of the 6 sc to form 6 petals. Slst to join.

Round 3: Holding petals forward, *ch4, working in the back of the petals, sc in between the petals* repeat from * to * around 5 more times.

Round 4: (Sc, hdc, 3dc, hdc, sc) work all these stitches in each of the ch4 loops. Slst to join.

Round 5: Repeat round 3.

Round 6: (Sc, hdc, 5dc, hdc, sc) work all these stitches in each of the ch4 loops. Slst to join. Do not fasten off yet. Continue on to make a leaf.

LEAF

Round 7: (Ch4, 2trc, ch2, sc in top of trc, 2trc, ch4, sc) work all these stitches in one stitch. Fasten off leaving a tail to sew with.

The instruction for the rose above is for the large rose, you can now make variations from this pattern to make smaller roses.

To make smaller roses you can just do rounds 1 and 2 and then add on leaf... or you can do rounds 1–4 and add one or two leaves... get creative!

Add pearl buttons or other embellishments to middle of roses if desired, or just leave plain.

Step 5: Working behind petals

Step 6: Leaf

Wrist-length Fingerless Gloves

*These very feminine gloves decorated with flowers and leaves
are a perfect touch for a summer wedding.*

Materials

- Aunt Lydia's size 10 crochet cotton
  – Color name White / 1 ball
- ⅛" elastic cord – 18" long x 2
- Decorative buttons
- Soft stretch elastic cord size 1/8in (about 3mm)
- Tapestry needle

- **Hook:** Steel hook size US 8 (1.25mm)

Skill level: Easy

Glossary of abbreviations

BL – backloop
ch – chain
dc – double crochet
dc slant stitch – slst in next st, ch3,
   2dc in same st
hdc – half double crochet
picot – ch3, 1slst in top of last sc
sc – single crochet
slst – slip stitch

GLOVES – Make 2
*Note: Cut approx. 6" of elastic cord,
(or length that comfortably fits around
wrist) overlap the ends approx. 1" and
sew ends together.*

Round 1: With White and size 8 steel
hook, work 60sc around entire elastic.
Slst to join. (60sc)
Round 2: Ch1, 1sc in the BL of the
same st as joining, 1sc in BL of each
sc around. Slst to join. (60sc)
You now are going to work in rows.
Ch3 counts as first dc.
Row 1: Ch3, 1dc in next sc, ch1, skip
next sc, 2dc in next 9sc, 1dc in next
sc, ch1, skip next sc, 1dc in next 2sc.
Turn.
Row 2: Ch3, 1dc in next dc, ch1, skip
next ch1, 1sc in next dc, (ch3, skip next

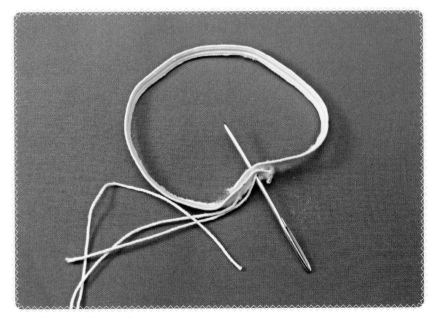

Step 1: Sew ends together

dc, 1sc in next dc) repeat 8 more times, ch1, skip next 1ch, 1dc in next dc, 1dc in top of ch3. Turn. (9 – ch3 loops)

Row 3: Ch3, 1dc in next dc, ch1, skip next 1ch1, 1sc in next ch3 loop, (ch3, 1sc in next ch3 loop) repeat 7 more times, ch1, skip next 1ch , 1dc in next dc, 1dc in top of ch3. Turn. (8 – ch3 loops)

Row 4: Ch3, 1dc in next dc, ch1, skip next 1ch, 1sc in next ch3 loop, (ch3, 1sc in next ch3 loop) repeat 6 more times, ch1, skip next 1ch, 1dc in next dc, 1dc in top of ch3. Turn. (7 – ch3 loops)

Row 5: Ch3, 1dc in next dc, ch1, skip next 1ch, 1sc in next ch3 loop, (ch3, 1sc in next ch3 loop) repeat 5 more times, ch1, skip next 1ch, 1dc in next dc, 1dc in top of ch3. Turn. (6 – ch3 loops)

Row 6: Ch3, 1dc in next dc, ch1, skip next 1ch, 1sc in next ch3 loop, (ch3, 1sc in next ch3 loop) repeat 4 more times, ch1, skip next 1ch, 1dc in next dc, 1dc in top of ch3. Turn. (5 – ch3 loops)

Row 7: Ch3, 1dc in next dc, ch1, skip next 1ch, 1sc in next ch3 loop, (ch3, 1sc in next ch3 loop) repeat 3 more times, ch1, skip next 1ch, 1dc in next dc, 1dc in top of ch3. Turn. (4 – ch3 loops)

Row 8: Ch3, 1dc in next dc, ch1, skip next 1ch, 1sc in next ch3 loop, (ch3, 1sc in next ch3 loop) repeat 2 more times, ch1, skip next 1ch, 1dc in next dc, 1dc in top of ch3. Turn. (3 – ch3 loops)

Row 9: Ch3, 1dc in next dc, ch1, skip next 1ch, 1sc in next ch3 loop, (ch3, 1sc in next ch3 loop) repeat 1 more time, ch1, skip next 1ch, 1dc in next dc, 1dc in top of ch3. Turn. (2 – ch3 loops)

Row 10: Ch3, 1dc in next dc, ch1, skip next 1ch, 1sc in next ch3 loop, ch3, 1sc in next ch3 loop, ch1, skip next 1ch, 1dc in next dc, 1dc in top of ch3. Turn. (1 – ch3 loop)

Row 11: Ch3, 1dc in next dc, ch1, skip next 1ch, 1sc in next ch3 loop, ch1, skip next 1ch, 1dc in next dc, 1dc in top of ch3. Turn.

Row 12: Ch18, 1sc in last ch3 to form finger loop. Turn.

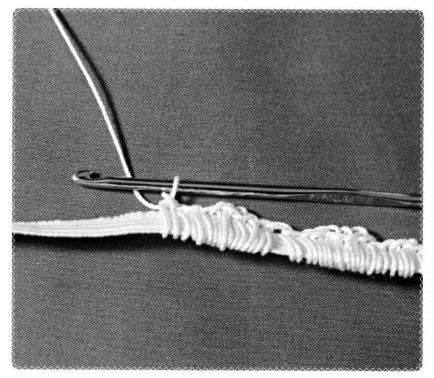

Step 2: Work over elastic

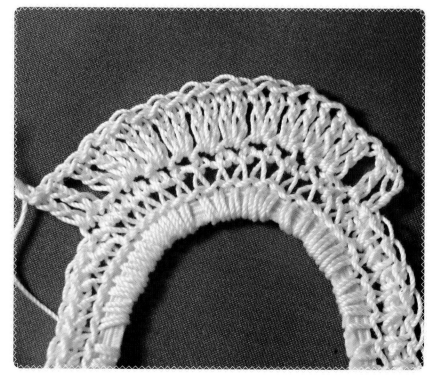

Step 3: Row 1

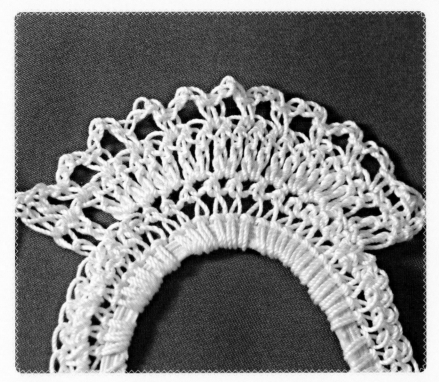

Step 4: Nine ch3 loops made

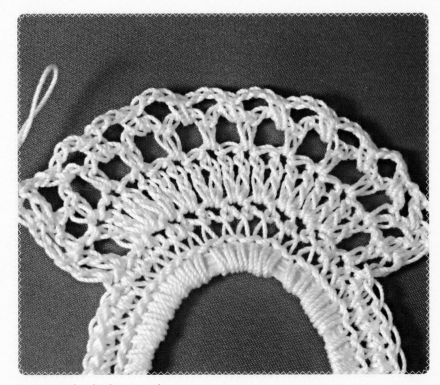

Step 5: Eight ch3 loops made

TRIM

Row 1: Push ch18 forward and working in the sc from row 12, slst in sc, ch3, 2dc in same sc, dc slant st in the space between 2dcs at end of each row of pineapple – and in every third sc on wristband. Slst to join. Fasten off and weave in ends.

WRIST

Round 1: With White and size 8 steel hook, and with right side facing you, fold down the slant stitches and attach cotton to the unworked loops of round 2, 1sc in each unworked loop around. Slst to join. (60sc)

Round 2: Ch1, 1sc in same st as joining, *ch3, skip next 2sc, 1sc in next sc* rep from * to * around. Slst to join. (20 – ch3 spaces)

Round 3: Ch1, 1sc in same st as joining, *2sc in ch3 loop, 1sc in next sc* rep from * to * around. Slst to join. (60sc)

Rounds 4–7: Repeat rounds 2 and 3 alternately.

Round 8: Ch3, 2dc in same st as joining, *skip next 2sc, dc slant st in next sc* rep from * to * around. Slst to join. Fasten off and weave in ends.

LEAF – Make 3

Round 1: With White and size 8 steel hook, ch8, 1sc in second ch from hook, 1hdc in next ch, 1dc in next 3ch, 1hdc in next ch, 2sc in last ch, picot, 1sc in same last ch. Now working on opposite side of ch, 1hdc in next ch, 1dc in next 3ch, 1hdc in next ch, 1sc in next ch. Slst to join.

Round 2: Ch1, 1slst in next 7sts, ch3, 1slst in next st, 1slst in each rem st around leaf. Slst to join. Fasten off leaving a tail to sew with. Put leaf aside for now.

FLOWER – Make 2

Row 1: With White and size 8 steel hook, ch15, 3dc in third ch from hook, 3dc in each rem ch. Turn.

Row 2: Ch1, (1sc, 1hdc, 1sc) in first dc, *1slst in next sc, (1sc, 1hdc, 1sc) in next sc* rep from * to * across. Fasten off leaving a long tail to sew with.

Roll stitches into a flower. Run a stitch through bottom of layers to hold flower shape. Sew leaf on back of flower. Sew flower to desired spot on glove.

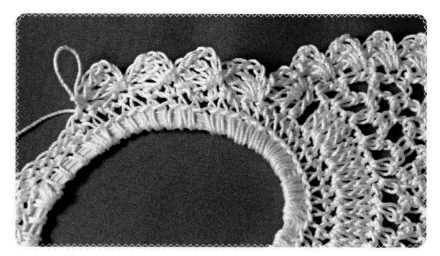

Step 6: Making trim

Step 7: Working in unworked loops from round 2

Step 8: Wrist cuff

Step 9: Leaf

Step 10: How to roll flower

Wedding Purse

Crochet lends itself to many types of designs and this lined wedding purse is no exception. Both beautiful and useful, you'll enjoy this purse for many years.

Materials

- Cascade Heritage Silk, 100gr (3.5 oz)/437yds (400 m), 85% Merino Superwash/15% Mulberry Silk
  – Color name Ivory / Color # 5618 / 1 skein
- Decorative buttons
- Yarn needle
- Decorative feathers and satin ribbons if desired

- **Hooks:** US D/3 (3.25mm) Susan Bates
  US F/5 (3.75mm) Susan Bates

Skill level: Easy

Purse measures 8½" tall x 9½" wide

Glossary of abbreviations

ch – chain
dc – double crochet
hdc – half double crochet
rep – repeat
sc – single crochet
slst – slip stitch
st – stitch
trc – treble crochet

BASE OF PURSE

Use 2 strands for rounds 1–5 only.
Round 1: With F hook, ch23, 2sc in second ch from hook, 1sc in next 20ch, 3sc in last ch. Now working on opposite side of ch, 1sc in next 20ch, 1sc in same ch as beg. Slst to join round. (46sc)
Round 2: Ch1, 2sc in same st as joining, 2sc in next sc, 1sc in next 20sc, 2sc in next 3sc, 1sc in next 20sc, 2sc in last sc. Slst to join round. (52sc)
Round 3: Ch1, 2sc in same st as joining, 1sc in next sc, 2sc in next sc, 1sc in next 21sc, (2sc in next sc, 1sc in next sc) rep 2 more times, 1sc in next 21sc, 2sc in next sc. Slst to join round. (58sc)
Round 4: Ch1, 2sc in same st as joining, 1sc in next 2sc, 2sc in next sc, 1sc in next 22sc, (2sc in next sc , 1sc in next 2sc) rep 2 more times, 1sc in next 22sc, 2sc in last sc. Slst to join round. (64sc)
Round 5: 1sc in same st as joining, 1sc in next sc, 2sc in next 3sc, 1sc in next

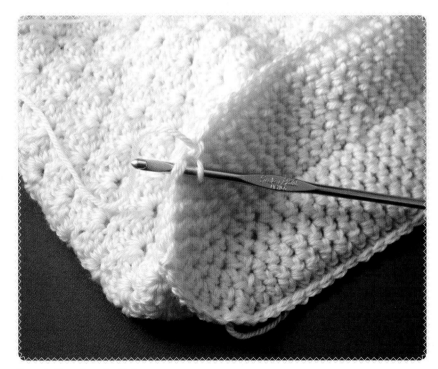

Step 1: Starting the lining

29sc, 2sc in next 3sc, 1sc in next 25sc, 2sc in last sc. Slst to join round. (70sc) Fasten off and weave in ends.

SIDES OF PURSE

Round 1: With D hook, attach yarn to front loop, where you fastened off, 1sc in same st as joining, 1sc in each front loop around. Slst to join round. (70sc)

Round 2: Ch1, 1sc in same st as joining, skip next sc, 5dc in next sc, skip next sc, 1sc in next sc, *skip next sc, 5dc in next sc, skip next sc, 1sc in next sc* rep from * to * around. You now are going to work in continuous rounds.

Round 3: 5dc in next sc, skip next 2dc *1sc in next dc, skip next 2dc, 5dc in next sc, skip next 2dc, 1sc in next dc, skip next 2dc* rep from * to * around. Continue working round 3 until purse measures approx. 7" high. Mark with stitch marker where your rounds started. NEXT: Skip next dc, 1sc in next dc, *1sc in next sc, (1sc in next dc, skip next dc) rep one more time, 1sc in next dc* rep from * to * around. Skip first sc, slst to next sc to join round. Fasten off and weave in ends. (73sc)

LINING

Round 1: With D hook, Turn purse inside out and attach yarn to any unworked loop from round 5 of base, 1sc in each unworked loop around. Slst to join round. (70sc)

Round 2: 1sc in each sc around and at the same time increase this round by 3sc anywhere on round. Slst to join round. (73sc)

Continue working 1sc in each sc around, until lining measures 7". Connecting Purse to Lining

Round 1: Holding lining next to outside of purse, matching scs, work 1sc in both layers to join them together. Slst to join round.

Step 2: Connecting the lining

Step 3: Working on flower

HANDLE

Rounds 1–4: 1sc in each sc around. Slst to join round. Ch1. (73sc)

Round 5: Depending on where you started the lining will determine where your holes go for the handles. Fold bag flat and find the center 15sc on each side of purse. Work 1sc in each sc around to where you have marked for first side of handle, ch15, skip next 15sc, 1sc in next 21sc, ch15,skip next 15sc, 1sc in each sc to end of round. Slst to join round.

Round 6: 1sc in each sc and in each ch around. Slst to join round. Fasten off and weave in ends.

FLOWER

Round 1: With Sand and D hook, ch 2, 6sc in second ch from hook. Slst to join. (6sc)

Round 2: (Sc, hdc, dc, hdc, sc) all in same st as joining, (sc, hdc, dc, hdc, sc) in each sc around, to form 6 petals. Slst to join.

Round 3: Holding petals forward, *ch3, working in the back of the petals, sc in between the petals* repeat around 5 more times

Round 4: (Sc, hdc, 3dc, hdc, sc) work all these stitches in each of the ch3 loops. Slst to join.

Round 5: Repeat round 3.

Round 6: (Sc, hdc, 5dc, hdc, sc) work all these stitches in each of the ch3 loops. Slst to join. Do not fasten off but continue on to stem.
Fasten off leaving a tail to sew with. Add embellishments to flower if desired.

STEM

Row 1: With D hook, ch3, 1dc in third ch from hook. Do not turn.

Row 2: Ch3, 1dc in between ch3 and dc from row 1. Do not turn.

Rows 3–10: Ch3, 1dc in between ch3 and dc from previous row. At the end of row 10 fasten off leaving a tail

Step 4: Tacking down stem of flower

to sew with. Add embellishment to flower if desired. Sew flower and stem to front of bag.

LEAF – Make 2

Round 1: With D hook, ch8, 1sc in second ch from hook, 1hdc in next ch, 1dc in next ch, 1trc in next ch, 1dc in next ch, 1hdc in next ch, 2sc in last ch, ch3, 1sc in same last ch.

Now working on opposite side of ch, and mirroring the stitches from the first side of leaf, 1hdc in next ch, 1dc in next ch, 1trc in next ch, 1dc in next ch, 1hdc in next ch, 1sc in next ch, slst to first sc to join round. Fasten off leaving a tail to sew with. Sew leaves onto stem in desired spots.

Ruffle Purse

Make this fun and flirty purse in your accent color from your wedding palette or use the suggestions made here.

Materials

- Cascade Sateen, 100% acrylic, #2 weight, 3.5oz/100g/300.7yds/275m
  – Color name Sand / Color # 22 / 2 skein
- Yarn needle
- **Hooks:** US F/5 (3.75mm) Susan Bates
  US G/6 (4.00mm) Susan Bates

Gauge: 22–24sc = 4"

Skill level: Intermediate

Measurements: 8" tall x 9½" wide

Glossary of abbreviations

BL – back loop
ch – chain
dc – double crochet
hdc – half double crochet
FL – front loop
sc – single crochet
slst – slip stitch
st – stitch
trc – treble crochet

Note: Ch3 counts as first dc.

BASE OF PURSE
Round 1: With G hook and Sand, ch23, 2sc in second ch from hook, 1sc in next 20ch, 3sc in last ch. Now working on opposite side of ch, 1sc in next 20ch, 1sc in same ch as beginning. Slst to join. (46sc)
Round 2: Ch1, 3sc in same st as joining, 1sc in next 22sc, 3sc in next sc, 1sc in next 22sc. Slst to join. (50sc)
Round 3: Ch1, 1sc in same st as joining, 3sc in next sc, 1sc in next 24sc, 3sc in next sc, 1sc in next 23sc. Slst to join. (54sc)
Round 4: Ch1, 1sc in same st as joining, 1sc in next sc, 3sc in next sc, 1sc in next 26sc, 3sc in next sc, 1sc in next 24sc. Slst to join. (58sc)
Round 5: Ch1, 1sc in same st as joining, 1sc in next 2sc, 3sc in next sc, 1sc in next 28sc, 3sc in next sc, 1sc in next 25sc. Slst to join. (62sc)
Round 6: Ch1, 1sc in FL of same st as

Step 1: Working in the front loop around base of purse

joining, 1sc in FL of each sc around. Slst to join.

BODY OF PURSE
Round 1: Ch3, 1dc in each sc around. Slst to join.
Round 2: Ch3, 1dc in each dc around. Slst to join.
Round 3: Ch3, 1dc in BL of each dc around. Slst to join.
Rounds 4–15: Repeat rounds 2 and 3 in sequence 6 more times. Ch2 turn.

RUFFLES
Round 1: With F hook and now work in the unworked loops from round that you worked BL in. Going straight down, next to ch3 line, 1sc in first unworked loop, ch1, *skip next unworked loop, 2dc in next loop, 3dc in next loop, 2dc in next 2 loops, ch1, skip next loop, 1sc in next loop, ch1* rep from * to * around, ending with skip last 3 loops. Slst to first dc to join round.
Round 2: Ch1, 1sc in same st as joining, 1sc in next dc, 1hdc in next dc, 1dc in next sc, (1dc, 1trc, 1dc) all in next dc, 1dc in next dc, 1hdc in next dc, 1sc in next 2dc, skip next ch, skip next sc, skip next ch1, *1sc in next 2dc, 1hdc in next dc, 1dc in next dc, (1dc, 1trc, 1dc) all in next dc, 1dc in next dc, 1hdc in next dc, 1sc in next 2dc, skip next ch1, skip next sc, skip next ch1* rep from * to * around. Slst to second sc to join round.
Round 3: Ch1, skip next sc, (1slst, ch1 in each st) to top of trc, 1slst in top of trc, ch4, 1slst in top of trc, *(1slst, ch1, in each st) to top of trc, 1slst in top of trc, ch4, slst in top of trc again* rep from * to * around . Slst to join. Ch2.
Rounds 4–21: Repeat rounds 1–3 in sequence 6 more times. Fasten off and weave in ends.

Step 2: Working in the back loop of each dc around

Step 3: Round 1 of ruffles

Step 4: Round 2 of ruffles

LINING INSIDE PURSE
Round 1: Turn purse down so you can see round 6, attach yarn to any unworked loops from round 6 on bottom of purse. 1sc in same st as joining, 1sc in each sc around. Work in continuous rounds until inside of purse is as tall as outside of purse. NEXT: Working through both parts of the purse, sc tog the inside and outside layers tog. Continue on to top of bag.

TOP OF BAG
Round 1: Ch4 (counts as first dc and ch1) *skip next sc, 1dc in next sc, ch1* repeat from * to * around. Slst to join. Ch1.
Round 2: 1sc in same st as joining, 6dc in next ch1sp, *skip next dc, 1sc in next ch1sp, skip next dc, 6dc in next ch1 sp* rep from * to * around. Fasten off and weave in ends.

DRAWSTRING TIE
Ch120, 1slst in second ch from hook, 1slst in each remaining ch. Fasten off, weave in ends.
Weave drawstring through holes left from round 3 from top of bag. Knot ends of tie together.

Step 5: Round 3 of ruffles

Step 6: Going straight down for next row of ruffles

Step 7: Working on the lining of the purse

Step 8: sc together the lining and the outside of bag

DISCARD

Acknowledgements

Yarns purchased at:
http://www.sageyarn.com
A C Moore Craft Store
Joann's Fabric Store
http://www.cascadeyarns.com

Pictures taken at:
Taft Cottage on the Megansett Bluff
Borderland State Park in Easton MA
Renaud Photography studio, Taunton MA

I want to thank my talented and beautiful daughter Christina Gannon for helping me to make this book — I couldn't have done it without you. I also want to thank Tara Renaud my wonderful photographer. You have made this experience a lot of fun and your photos are gorgeous! I want to express my thanks to Bob and Debra Taft who own the Taft Cottage on the Megansett bluff. Thank you for graciously opening your home to us so we could get so many lovely pictures. Thank you to my husband for all of his help, support, and patience while I was busy writing the manuscript. I want to give a big thank-you to all the wonderful models that stood for hours in the cold and let us take their pictures. Everyone did a great job of modeling for us. Lastly, I want to thank Valerie Belsky and Cindy Kasabian for all their prayers and kind words of encouragement.